Praying For Your Children Made Easy

IYINOLUWA KUTI

Dedication

This book is created with love, faith, and hope for the next generation and those dedicated to leading children to God's light. I pray that this book will be a loving companion and an eternal source of courage and inspiration for parents and guardians who work tirelessly to instill God's love in their families, during times of joy and challenge.

Acknowledgments

I want to thank God for His unwavering guidance and presence in my life as I wrote this book. I want to thank my wonderful husband, beautiful children, and family for always being a source of joy and inspiration. Your love and support gave me the courage to write this book.

I am very grateful for the different children's ministries I have served since I was a teenager. The children I met in these ministries sparked my desire to establish God's love in the lives of young people. I want to thank everyone who contributed to making this book a reality; I appreciate your expertise and efforts.

Finally, thank all parents, guardians, and families who guide their children through prayer and the Word of God. This book will be a valuable resource for your family's spiritual journey.

Table of Contents

Introduction

❖

Raising children is one of life's most significant and demanding experiences. As parents, we are responsible for guiding our children through life's various stages, helping them grow into well-rounded individuals who walk with faith, integrity, and purpose. Prayer is one of our most effective weapons in this prestigious calling. At the same time, with its endless knowledge and comfort, the Bible supplies us with verses that can form the foundation of our prayers for our children's lives. By praying these verses over our children, we can cover every aspect of their lives with God's powerful word, urging Him to guide, protect, and bless them.

"Praying for Your Children Made Easy" is a collection of carefully chosen Bible verses that address essential stages in your child's development. This book is organized into sections about faith, protection, wisdom, health, relationships, and the future. Each verse is personalized, allowing you to pray for your child's path.

Whether you are a parent, grandparent, guardian, or mentor, this book offers a biblical framework for praying over your children, ensuring that every aspect of their lives is grounded in God's Word. As you begin these prayers, realize that God's promises are unbreakable, that He has infinite power, and trust that God's active and living word will profoundly impact your family. Amen.

CHAPTER 1:

Prayers for Faith

❖

Faith is the foundation of our connection with God. As
parents, one of our most fundamental responsibilities
is to help our children establish a solid foundation in
faith. Praying for your children's faith will help them
get closer to God, grasp His word, and believe His
promises. Below are personalized Bible verses to pray
over your children's faith journey.

BIBLE VERSES

1. Ephesians 3:17-19

"So that Christ may dwell in your hearts through faith. And I pray that you, being rooted and established in love, may have power, together with all the Lord's holy people, to grasp how wide and long and high and deep is the love of Christ and to know this love that surpasses knowledge, that you may be filled to the measure of all the fullness of God."

Prayer:

"Lord, may You dwell in the heart of [Child's Name] by faith. Let [him/her] be rooted and established in Your love, comprehending the breadth of Your love and being filled with Your fullness." Amen.

2. Romans 10:17

"Consequently, faith comes from hearing the message, and the message is heard through the word about Christ."

Prayer:

"Father, let [Child's Name] hear Your message and grow in faith through the word of Christ." Amen.

3. Hebrews 11:1

"Now faith is confidence in what we hope for and assurance about what we do not see."

Prayer:
"God, grant [Child's Name] the confidence and assurance that comes from true faith, believing in Your promises even when they are not seen." Amen.

---

4. James 1:5

"If any of you lacks wisdom, you should ask God, who gives generously to all without finding fault, and it will be given to you."

Prayer:
"Lord, I pray that whenever [Child's Name] lacks wisdom, [he/she] will turn to You. Grant [him/her] the wisdom [he/she] seeks generously." Amen.

---

5. Proverbs 3:5-6

"Trust in the LORD with all your heart and lean not on your own understanding; in all your ways submit to him, and he will make your paths straight."

Prayer:
"Father, help [Child's Name] to trust in You with all [his/her] heart and not rely on [his/her] own understanding. Guide [him/her] in every aspect of life, making [his/her] paths straight." Amen.

---

6. Psalm 32:8

"I will instruct you and teach you in the way you should go; I will counsel you with my loving eye on you."

Prayer:

"God, instruct and teach [Child's Name] in the way [he/she] should go. Counsel [him/her] with Your loving eye and guidance." Amen.

---

7. Colossians 2:6-7

"So then, just as you received Christ Jesus as Lord, continue to live your lives in him, rooted and built up in him, strengthened in the faith as you were taught, and overflowing with thankfulness."

Prayer:

"Lord, may [Child's Name] continue to live [his/her] life in You, being rooted and built up in You, strengthened in the faith, and overflowing with thankfulness." Amen.

---

8. 1 Timothy 4:12

"Do not let anyone look down on you because you are young, but set an example for the believers in speech, in conduct, in love, in faith, and in purity."

Prayer:

"Father, let [Child's Name] set an example for others in speech, conduct, love, faith, and purity, despite [his/her] young age." Amen.

---

9. Matthew 17:20

"He replied because you have so little faith. Truly, I tell you, if you have faith as small as a mustard seed, you can say to this mountain, move from here to there, and it will move. Nothing will be impossible for you."

Prayer:

"Jesus, may [Child's Name] have faith even as small as a mustard seed, knowing that nothing will be impossible with such faith." Amen.

---

10. Galatians 2:20

"I have been crucified with Christ, and I no longer live, but Christ lives in me. The life I now live in the body, I live by faith in the Son of God, who loved me and gave himself for me."

Prayer:

"Lord, help [Child's Name] to live by faith in the Son of God, who loved [him/her] and gave Himself for [him/her]." Amen.

---

11. Mark 9:24

"Immediately, the boy's father exclaimed, I do believe; help me overcome my unbelief!"

Prayer:

"Father, support [Child's Name] in overcoming unbelief. Strengthen [his/her] faith in You." Amen.

12. 1 Peter 1:8-9

"Though you have not seen him, you love him, and even though you do not see him now, you believe in him and are filled with an inexpressible and glorious joy, for you are receiving the end result of your faith, the salvation of your souls."

Prayer:

"God, may [Child's Name], even without seeing You, believe in You and be filled with inexpressible and glorious joy, knowing the salvation of [his/her] soul." Amen.

---

13. John 20:29

"Then Jesus told him, Because you have seen me, you have believed; blessed are those who have not seen and yet have believed."

Prayer:

"Jesus, bless [Child's Name] as [he/she] believes in You even without seeing." Amen.

---

14. Isaiah 7:9b

"If you do not stand firm in your faith, you will not stand at all."

Prayer:

"Lord, help [Child's Name] to stand firm in [his/her] faith so that [he/she] may stand strong in all aspects of life." Amen.

---

15. 2 Corinthians 5:7

"For we live by faith, not by sight."

Prayer:

"God, teach [Child's Name] to live by faith and not by sight, trusting in Your divine guidance." Amen.

---

16. Matthew 21:21

"Jesus replied, Truly I tell you, if you have faith and do not doubt, not only can you do what was done to the fig tree, but also you can say to this mountain, Go, throw yourself into the sea, and it will be done."

Prayer:

"Jesus, grant [Child's Name] a faith that does not doubt, so [he/she] can do extraordinary things through You." Amen.

---

17. 1 Corinthians 16:13

"Be on your guard; stand firm in the faith; be courageous; be strong."

Prayer:

"Lord, may [Child's Name] always be on guard, stand firm in the faith, be courageous, and be strong in You." Amen.

---

18. Psalm 16:8

"I keep my eyes always on the LORD. With him at my right hand, I will not be shaken."

Prayer:

"Father, help [Child's Name] to keep [his/her] eyes always on You. May [he/she] never be shaken with You by [his/her] side." Amen.

19. 1 John 5:4

"For everyone born of God overcomes the world. This is the victory that has overcome the world, even our faith."

Prayer:

"God, let [Child's Name] find victory and overcome the world through [his/her] faith in You." Amen.

20. Hebrews 12:2

"Fixing our eyes on Jesus, the pioneer and perfecter of faith. For the joy set before him, he endured the cross, scorning its shame, and sat down at the right hand of the throne of God."

Prayer:

"Lord, help [Child's Name] fix [his/her] eyes on Jesus, the pioneer and perfecter of faith. May [he/she] find joy and strength in [his/her] faith journey." Amen.

21. Matthew 19:14

"But Jesus said, Let the little children come to me and do not hinder them, for to such belongs the kingdom of heaven."

Prayer:

Dear Jesus, draw [Child's Name] close to You. May [he/she] come to know You profoundly and personally, understanding that [he/she] is cherished in Your kingdom. Amen.

---

22. Psalm 23:1

"The Lord is my shepherd; I shall not want."

Prayer:

God Almighty, guide and protect [Child's Name]. Let [Him/Her] lack no good thing under Your care, finding peace and contentment in You. Amen.

Conclusion

Personalizing these Bible verses enables you to pray for your children's faith with greater depth. Remember, prayer is an excellent tool for shaping and strengthening one's spiritual life. Continue to pray for them, confident that God will nourish and build their faith as they follow Him.

Prayer Journals and Reflections
(Write your ideas, requests, and any revelations you receive)

CHAPTER 2

Prayers for Protection and Safety

◈

One of our most pressing concerns is the safety and protection of our children, and God's Word gives us powerful verses from which to pray over their lives. These verses remind us to put our trust in God's ever-present care.

1. Psalm 91:11

"For He will command His angels concerning you to guard you in all your ways."

Prayer:

"Lord, command Your angels to guard [Child's Name] in all [his/her] ways, keeping [him/her] safe and secure." Amen.

2. Proverbs 18:10

"The name of the LORD is a fortified tower; the righteous run to it and are safe."

Prayer:

"Heavenly Father, may [Child's Name] always run to You, finding safety and refuge in Your name." Amen.

3. Isaiah 41:10

"So do not fear, for I am with you; do not be dismayed, for I am your God. I will strengthen you and help you; I will uphold you with my righteous right hand."

Prayer:

"God, let [Child's Name] know that You are with [him/her], alleviating fear and dismay. Strengthen and uphold [him/her] with Your righteous hand." Amen.

4. Psalm 121:7-8

"The LORD will keep you from all harm—He will watch over your life; the LORD will watch over your coming and going both now and forevermore."

Prayer:

"Lord, keep [Child's Name] from all harm. Watch over [his/her] life, [his/her] coming and going, both now and always." Amen.

---

5. Psalm 91:4

"He will cover you with His feathers, and under His wings, you will find refuge; His faithfulness will be your shield and rampart."

Prayer:

"Heavenly Father, cover [Child's Name] with Your feathers. Let [him/her] find refuge under Your wings, and let Your faithfulness be [his/her] shield and rampart." Amen.

---

6. Psalm 46:1

"God is our refuge and strength, an ever-present help in trouble."

Prayer:

"God, be [Child's Name] 's refuge and strength, an ever-present help in trouble. May [he/she] always find solace in You." Amen.

---

7. Psalm 34:7

"The angel of the LORD encamps around those who fear Him, and He delivers them."

Prayer:

"Lord, let Your angel encamp around [Child's Name] and deliver [him/her] from all harm." Amen.

---

8. 2 Thessalonians 3:3

"But the Lord is faithful, and He will strengthen you and protect you from the evil one."

Prayer:

"Father, strengthen and protect [Child's Name] from the evil one, showcasing Your faithfulness." Amen.

---

9. Psalm 138:7

"Though I walk in the midst of trouble, You preserve my life. You stretch out Your hand against the anger of my foes; with Your right hand, You save me."

Prayer:

"Lord, even when [Child's Name] walks through adversity, protect [his/her] life. Stretch forth Your right hand to save [him/her] from his/her foes. Amen.

---

10. John 17:15

"My prayer is not that You take them out of the world but that You protect them from the evil one."

Prayer:

"Heavenly Father, protect [Child's Name] from the evil one, even as [he/she] navigates this world." Amen.

11. Deuteronomy 31:6

"Be strong and courageous. Do not be afraid or terrified because of them, for the LORD your God goes with you; He will never leave you nor forsake you."

Prayer:

"Lord, grant [Child's Name] strength and courage. Let [him/her] not be afraid, knowing that You go with [him/her] and will never leave nor forsake [him/her]." Amen.

12. Proverbs 3:24

"When you lie down, you will not be afraid; when you lie down, your sleep will be sweet."

Prayer:

"Father, when [Child's Name] lies down, let [him/her] not be afraid. Grant [him/her] sweet and peaceful sleep." Amen.

13. Isaiah 43:2

"When you pass through the waters, I will be with you, and when you pass through the rivers, they will not sweep over you. When you walk through the fire, you will not be burned; the flames will not set you ablaze."

Prayer:

"God, be with [Child's Name] as [he/she] passes through life's waters and rivers. May [he/she] not be swept away or burned, knowing Your presence protects [him/her]." Amen.

14. Psalm 23:4

"Even though I walk through the darkest valley, I will fear no evil, for You are with me; Your rod and Your staff, they comfort me."

Prayer:

"Lord, when [Child's Name] walks through the darkest valleys, let [him/her] fear no evil. Comfort [him/her] with Your rod and staff." Amen.

15. Matthew 6:13

"And lead us not into temptation, but deliver us from the evil one."

Prayer:

"Father, lead [Child's Name] not into temptation, but deliver [him/her] from the evil one." Amen.

16. Psalm 91:1

"Whoever dwells in the shelter of the Most High will rest in the shadow of the Almighty."

Prayer:

"Lord, may [Child's Name] dwell in the shelter of the Most High and rest in the shadow of the Almighty." Amen.

---

17. 2 Samuel 22:3-4

"My God is my rock, in whom I take refuge, my shield and the horn of my salvation. He is my stronghold, my refuge, and my savior— from violent people. You save me."

Prayer:

"God, be [Child's Name] 's rock, refuge, and shield. Save [him/her] from violent people and protect [him/her] with Your salvation." Amen.

---

18. Nahum 1:7

"The LORD is good, a refuge in times of trouble. He cares for those who trust in Him."

Prayer:

"Lord, be a refuge for [Child's Name] in times of trouble. Show [him/her] Your care as [he/she] places trust in You." Amen.

---

19. Psalm 5:11

"But let all who take refuge in You be glad; let them ever sing for joy. Spread Your protection over them, that those who love Your name may rejoice in You."

Prayer:

"Father, let [Child's Name] take refuge in You and be glad. Spread Your protection over [him/her], so [he/she] may rejoice in Your name." Amen.

20. 2 Timothy 4:18

"The Lord will rescue me from every evil attack and will bring me safely to His heavenly kingdom. To Him be glory forever and ever. Amen."

Prayer:

"Lord, rescue [Child's Name] from every evil attack and bring [him/her] safely to Your heavenly kingdom. To You be glory forever and ever. Amen."

Conclusion

Praying these personalized Bible verses over your children provides divine protection while reinforcing your confidence in God's promises. Trust that the Lord hears every prayer and is ever-present to protect your lovely children.

Prayer Journals and Reflections
(Write your ideas, requests, and any revelations you receive)

CHAPTER 3

Prayers for Wisdom and Guidance

Wisdom and guidance are crucial as our children make life's numerous decisions. Seeking God's direction and counsel is essential for making sound and informed judgments. Praying these scriptures over your children will help them develop greater insight and discernment.

BIBLE VERSES

1. James 1:5

"If any of you lacks wisdom, you should ask God, who gives generously to all without finding fault, and it will be given to you."

Prayer:

"Lord, whenever [Child's Name] lacks wisdom, let [him/her] turn to You. Grant [him/her] the wisdom [he/she] seeks generously." Amen.

2. Proverbs 3:5-6

"Trust in the LORD with all your heart and lean not on your own understanding; in all your ways submit to him, and he will make your paths straight."

Prayer:

"Father, help [Child's Name] to trust in You with all [his/her] heart and not rely on [his/her] own understanding. Guide [him/her] in every aspect of life, making [his/her] paths straight." Amen.

3. Psalm 32:8

"I will instruct you and teach you in the way you should go; I will counsel you with my loving eye on you."

Prayer:

"God, instruct and teach [Child's Name] in the way [he/she] should go. Counsel [him/her] with Your loving eye and guidance." Amen.

4. Proverbs 2:6

"For the LORD gives wisdom; from His mouth come knowledge and understanding."

Prayer:
"Father, give [Child's Name] wisdom, knowledge, and understanding from Your mouth as [he/she] learns and grows." Amen.

---

5. Colossians 1:9

"For this reason, since the day we heard about you, we have not stopped praying for you. We continually ask God to fill you with the knowledge of his will through all the wisdom and understanding that the Spirit gives."

Prayer:
"Lord, I continually ask that You fill [Child's Name] with the knowledge of Your will through all the wisdom and understanding that Your Spirit gives." Amen.

---

6. Proverbs 4:7

"The beginning of wisdom is this: Get wisdom. Though it cost all you have, get understanding."

Prayer:
"Father, instill a heart that seeks wisdom in [Child's Name]. May [he/she] gain understanding no matter the cost." Amen.

---

7. Ecclesiastes 7:12

"Wisdom is a shelter as money is a shelter, but the advantage of knowledge is this: Wisdom preserves those who have it."

Prayer:

"Lord, let wisdom be a shelter for [Child's Name] and preserve [him/her] through [his/her] understanding." Amen.

8. Psalm 119:105

"Your word is a lamp for my feet, a light on my path."

Prayer:

"Father, may Your word be a lamp for [Child's Name] 's feet and a light on [his/her] path, guiding [him/her] in all decisions." Amen.

9. Jeremiah 29:11

"For I know the plans I have for you, declares the LORD, plans to prosper you and not to harm you, plans to give you hope and a future."

Prayer:

"Lord, reveal Your plans to [Child's Name], plans to prosper [him/her] and not to harm [him/her], plans to give [him/her] hope and a future." Amen.

10. Proverbs 16:16

"How much better to get wisdom than gold, to get insight rather than silver!"

Prayer:
"God, help [Child's Name] understand that gaining wisdom and insight is far better than acquiring gold and silver." Amen.

---

11. Isaiah 30:21

"Whether you turn to the right or to the left, your ears will hear a voice behind you, saying, 'This is the way; walk in it.'"

Prayer:
"Lord, let [Child's Name] hear Your voice guiding [him/her], saying, 'This is the way; walk in it,' whenever [he/she] turns to the right or the left." Amen.

---

12. Ephesians 5:15-16

"Be very careful, then, how you live—not as unwise but as wise, making the most of every opportunity, because the days are evil."

Prayer:
"Father, help [Child's Name] live wisely, making the most of every opportunity, recognizing that the days are evil." Amen.

---

13. Proverbs 1:7

"The fear of the LORD is the beginning of knowledge, but fools despise wisdom and instruction."

Prayer:

"Lord, let [Child's Name] have a healthy fear of You, recognizing that it is the beginning of knowledge. May [he/she] not despise wisdom and instruction." Amen.

---

14. Colossians 2:2-3

"My goal is that they may be encouraged in heart and united in love, so that they may have the full riches of complete understanding, in order that they may know the mystery of God, namely, Christ, in whom are hidden all the treasures of wisdom and knowledge."

Prayer:

"God, encourage [Child's Name] in heart and unite [him/her] in love so that [he/she] may have complete understanding and know Christ, in whom all the treasures of wisdom and knowledge are hidden." Amen.

---

15. Daniel 1:17

"To these four young men, God gave knowledge and understanding of all kinds of literature and learning. And Daniel could understand visions and dreams of all kinds."

Prayer:

"Lord, grant [Child's Name] the knowledge and understanding needed for all areas of [his/her] studies, just as You did for Daniel." Amen.

---

16. 1 Kings 3:9

"So give your servant a discerning heart to govern your people and to distinguish between right and wrong."

Prayer:

"Father, give [Child's Name] a discerning heart to distinguish between right and wrong, guiding [him/her] in wisdom." Amen.

17. Proverbs 13:20

"Walk with the wise and become wise, for a companion of fools suffers harm."

Prayer:

"Lord, help [Child's Name] to walk with the wise and become wise. Keep [him/her] away from companions who might lead [him/her] to harm." Amen.

18. Romans 12:2

"Do not conform to the pattern of this world, but be transformed by the renewing of your mind. Then you will be able to test and approve what God's will is—his good, pleasing, and perfect will."

Prayer:

"God, let [Child's Name] not conform to the patterns of this world. Transform [him/her] by renewing [his/her] mind so that [he/she] may understand and follow Your good, pleasing, and perfect will." Amen.

19. 2 Timothy 3:15

"...and how from infancy you have known the Holy Scriptures, which are able to make you wise for salvation through faith in Christ Jesus."

Prayer:

"Lord, let [Child's Name] grow in the knowledge of the Holy Scriptures from an early age, making [him/her] wise for salvation through faith in Christ Jesus." Amen.

20. Isaiah 28:29

"All this also comes from the LORD Almighty, whose plan is wonderful, whose wisdom is magnificent."

Prayer:

"Father, may [Child's Name] recognize that wisdom and excellence come from You, whose plan is wonderful and wisdom is magnificent." Amen.

21. Philippians 1:9-10

"And it is my prayer that your love may abound more and more, with knowledge and all discernment, so that you may approve what is excellent, and so be pure and blameless for the day of Christ."

Prayer:

Loving Father, may [Child's Name's] love overflow, accompanied by knowledge and discernment. Help [him/her] to choose what is excellent and remain pure before You. Amen.

Conclusion

By praying these personalized Bible verses over your children, you give them the vital gift of God's wisdom and guidance. Trust that the Lord will shape their hearts and minds, giving them the insight they need to navigate life's challenges.

Prayer Journals and Reflections
(Write your ideas, requests, and any revelations you receive)

CHAPTER 4

Prayers for Health and Wellness

—◇—

Our children's physical and mental well-being is another essential part of our prayers. These verses remind us of God's healing ability and desire for our well-being. Use these personalized Bible verses to pray for your children's health and well-being, believing God will bring healing and wholeness into their lives.

1. Jeremiah 30:17

"For I will restore health to you and heal you of your wounds, says the LORD."

Prayer:

"Lord, restore health to [Child's Name] and heal [his/her] wounds. Let Your healing touch be upon [him/her]." Amen.

2. Isaiah 53:5

"But He was wounded for our transgressions, He was bruised for our iniquities; The chastisement for our peace was upon Him, and by His stripes we are healed."

Prayer:

"Jesus, thank You for the sacrifice You made. May [Child's Name] be healed and made whole by Your stripes." Amen.

3. 3 John 1:2

"Dear friend, I pray that you may enjoy good health and that all may go well with you, even as your soul is getting along well."

Prayer:

"Loving Father, I pray for [Child's Name] 's good health. May [he/she] thrive physically, emotionally, and spiritually." Amen.

4. Psalm 103:2-3

"Praise the LORD, my soul, and forget not all His benefits—who forgives all your sins and heals all your diseases."

Prayer:
"Lord, let [Child's Name] praise You and remember all Your benefits. Heal [him/her] of all diseases and forgive [his/her] sins." Amen.

5. Proverbs 3:7-8

"Do not be wise in your own eyes; fear the LORD and shun evil. This will bring health to your body and nourishment to your bones."

Prayer:
"Father, help [Child's Name] not to be wise in [his/her] own eyes. May [he/she] fear You and shun evil, bringing health to [his/her] body and nourishment to [his/her] bones." Amen.

6. James 5:14-15

"Is anyone among you sick? Let them call the elders of the church to pray over them and anoint them with oil in the name of the Lord. And the prayer offered in faith will make the sick person well; the Lord will raise them up."

Prayer:
"Lord, whenever [Child's Name] is sick, may we call upon the elders to pray over [him/her]. Let the prayer offered in faith make [him/her] well and raise [him/her] up." Amen.

7. Psalm 147:3

"He heals the brokenhearted and binds up their wounds."

Prayer:

"God, heal [Child's Name] 's broken heart and bind up [his/her] wounds with Your loving care." Amen.

8. Exodus 23:25

"Worship the LORD your God, and His blessing will be on your food and water. I will take away sickness from among you."

Prayer:

"Heavenly Father, as [Child's Name] worships You, bless [his/her] food and water, and take away sickness from [him/her]." Amen.

9. Psalm 41:3

"The LORD sustains them on their sickbed and restores them from their bed of illness."

Prayer:

"Lord, sustain [Child's Name] on [his/her] sickbed and restore [him/her] from [his/her] illness." Amen.

10. Isaiah 58:8

"Then your light will break forth like the dawn, and your healing will quickly appear; then your righteousness will go before you, and the glory of the LORD will be your rear guard."

Prayer:

"Lord, let [Child's Name] 's light break forth like the dawn and [his/her] healing quickly appear. May Your righteousness go before [him/her], and Your glory be [his/her] rear guard." Amen.

11. Proverbs 4:20-22

"My son, pay attention to what I say; turn your ear to my words. Do not let them out of your sight; keep them within your heart, for they are life to those who find them and health to one's whole body."

Prayer:

"Father, help [Child's Name] pay attention to Your words and keep them in [his/her] heart. May they bring life and health to [his/her] whole body." Amen.

12. Jeremiah 33:6

"'Nevertheless, I will bring health and healing to it; I will heal my people and will let them enjoy abundant peace and security."

Prayer:

"Lord, bring health and healing to [Child's Name]. Let [him/her] enjoy abundant peace and security." Amen.

13. Matthew 8:16-17

"When evening came, many who were demon-possessed were brought to Him, and He drove out the spirits with a word and healed all the sick. This was to fulfill what was spoken through the prophet Isaiah: He took up our infirmities and bore our diseases."

Prayer:
"Jesus, thank You for taking up [Child's Name] 's infirmities and bearing [his/her] diseases. Heal [him/her] completely as You did in times past." Amen.

14. Psalm 30:2

"LORD my God, I called to you for help, and you healed me."

Prayer:
"Lord my God, as [Child's Name] calls to You for help, heal [him/her] and make [him/her] whole." Amen.

15. Deuteronomy 7:15

"The LORD will keep you free from every disease. He will not inflict on you the horrible diseases you knew in Egypt, but he will inflict them on all who hate you."

Prayer:
"Lord, keep [Child's Name] free from every disease. Protect [him/her] from any affliction." Amen.

16. Mark 5:34

"He said to her, 'Daughter, your faith has healed you. Go in peace and be freed from your suffering.'"

Prayer:
"Jesus, let [Child's Name] 's faith bring healing. Grant [him/her] peace and freedom from suffering." Amen.

---

17. Psalm 6:2

"Have mercy on me, LORD, for I am faint; heal me, LORD, for my bones are in agony."

Prayer:
"Lord, have mercy on [Child's Name] when [he/she] feels faint. Heal [him/her] and relieve [his/her] agony." Amen.

---

18. 1 Peter 2:24

"He himself bore our sins in his body on the tree, that we might die to sin and live to righteousness. By his wounds, you have been healed."

Prayer:
"Jesus, thank You for bearing [Child's Name] 's sins on the cross. By Your wounds, may [he/she] be healed and live in righteousness." Amen.

---

19. Psalm 107:20

"He sent out his word and healed them; He rescued them from the grave."

Prayer:

"Father, send out Your word and heal [Child's Name]. Rescue [him/her] from any danger or illness." Amen.

---

20. Malachi 4:2

"But for you who fear my name, the sun of righteousness shall rise with healing in its wings. You shall go out leaping like calves from the stall."

Prayer:

"Lord, may the sun of righteousness rise with healing in its wings for [Child's Name]. Let [him/her] go out with joy and health, leaping like calves from the stall." Amen.

Conclusion

Praying these personalized Bible verses over your children allows God's healing power to enter their lives. Trust in His promises and pray for your children, knowing that the Lord is greatly concerned about their well-being.

Prayer Journals and Reflections
(Write your ideas, requests, and any revelations you receive)

Prayers for Education and Learning

✦ ◇ ✦

Education and learning are essential components of your child's development. Praying for their academic journey can help them get divine guidance, knowledge, and perseverance. Using these verses to pray for your children to be intelligent, inquiring, and open to new ideas will help create a solid basis for their long-term development.

BIBLE VERSES

1. Proverbs 2:6

"For the LORD gives wisdom; from His mouth come knowledge and understanding."

Prayer:

"Father, give [Child's Name] wisdom, knowledge, and understanding directly from Your mouth as [he/she] embarks on [his/her] journey." Amen.

2. Daniel 1:17

"To these four young men, God gave knowledge and understanding of all kinds of literature and learning. And Daniel could understand visions and dreams of all kinds."

Prayer:

"Lord, grant [Child's Name] the knowledge and understanding needed for all areas of [his/her] studies, just as You did for Daniel." Amen.

3. Proverbs 9:10

"The fear of the LORD is the beginning of wisdom, and knowledge of the Holy One is understanding."

Prayer:

"God, instill in [Child's Name] a healthy fear of You, which is the beginning of wisdom. May [he/she] gain knowledge and understanding of You, the Holy One." Amen.

4. James 1:5

"If any of you lacks wisdom, you should ask God, who gives generously to all without finding fault, and it will be given to you."

Prayer:

"Lord, whenever [Child's Name] lacks wisdom, let [him/her] turn to You. Grant [him/her] the wisdom [he/she] seeks generously." Amen.

---

5. Proverbs 1:5

"Let the wise listen and add to their learning, and let the discerning get guidance."

Prayer:

"Father, help [Child's Name] to listen and add to [his/her] learning. May [he/she] be discerning and get the guidance needed." Amen.

---

6. 2 Timothy 2:7

"Reflect on what I am saying, for the Lord will give you insight into all this."

Prayer:

"Lord, as [Child's Name] studies, allow [him/her] to reflect on the material and grant [him/her] insight into all subjects.

---

7. Psalm 119:18

"Open my eyes that I may see wonderful things in your law."

Prayer:

"Father, open [Child's Name] 's eyes to see wonderful things in Your teachings and apply them to [his/her] learning journey." Amen.

---

8. Job 12:13

"To God belong wisdom and power; counsel and understanding are his."

Prayer:

"God, may [Child's Name] recognize that wisdom, power, counsel, and understanding belong to You. Let [him/her] seek all from You." Amen.

---

9. Proverbs 4:7

"The beginning of wisdom is this: Get wisdom. Though it cost all you have, get understanding."

Prayer:

"Lord, instill in [Child's Name] a deep desire to seek wisdom and understanding, no matter the cost." Amen.

---

10. Psalm 25:4-5

"Show me your ways, LORD, teach me your paths. Guide me in your truth and teach me, for you are God my Savior, and my hope is in you all day long."

Prayer:

"Father, show [Child's Name] Your ways and teach [him/her] Your paths. Guide [him/her] in Your truth and be [his/her] hope." Amen.

11. Psalm 32:8

"I will instruct you and teach you in the way you should go; I will counsel you with my loving eye on you."

Prayer:

"God, instruct and teach [Child's Name] in the way [he/she] should go. Counsel [him/her] with Your loving eye and guidance." Amen.

12. Colossians 2:6-7

"So then, just as you received Christ Jesus as Lord, continue to live your lives in him, rooted and built up in him, strengthened in the faith as you were taught, and overflowing with thankfulness."

Prayer:

"Lord, may [Child's Name] continue to live [his/her] life in You, being rooted and built up in You, strengthened in faith and overflowing with thankfulness." Amen.

13. Philippians 1:9-10

"And this is my prayer: that your love may abound more and more in knowledge and depth of insight so that you may be able to discern what is best and may be pure and blameless for the day of Christ."

Prayer:

"Father, let [Child's Name] 's love abound more and more in knowledge and depth of insight, helping [him/her] to discern what is best." Amen.

14. Ephesians 1:17-18

"I keep asking that the God of our Lord Jesus Christ, the glorious Father, may give you the Spirit of wisdom and revelation so that you may know him better. I pray that the eyes of your heart may be enlightened in order that you may know the hope to which he has called you, the riches of his glorious inheritance in his holy people."

Prayer:

"Lord, give [Child's Name] the Spirit of wisdom and revelation so that [he/she] might better know You. Enlighten [Child's Name]'s heart to understand the hope to which You have called [him/her]." Amen.

15. Proverbs 2:10-11

"For wisdom will enter your heart, and knowledge will be pleasant to your soul. Discretion will protect you, and understanding will guard you."

Prayer:

"Father, let wisdom enter [Child's Name] 's heart and make knowledge pleasant to [him/her] soul. Grant [him/her] discretion and understanding for protection and guidance." Amen.

16. Colossians 3:16

"Let the message of Christ dwell among you richly as you teach and admonish one another with all wisdom through psalms, hymns, and songs from the Spirit, singing to God with gratitude in your hearts."

Prayer:

"Lord, may the message of Christ dwell richly in [Child's Name]. Let [him/her] teach and admonish others with wisdom and gratitude in [his/her] heart." Amen.

---

17. Psalms 119:66

"Teach me good judgment and knowledge, for I believe your commandments."

Prayer:

"God, teach [Child's Name] good judgment and knowledge. Help [him/her] to believe and follow Your commandments in all that [he/she] learns." Amen.

---

18. Romans 12:2

"Do not conform to the pattern of this world, but be transformed by the renewing of your mind. Then you will be able to test and approve what God's will is—His good, pleasing, and perfect will."

Prayer:

"Father, help [Child's Name] not conform to this world, but be transformed by renewing [his/her] mind, so [he/she] may know the good, pleasing, and perfect will of God." Amen.

---

19. Colossians 2:2-3

"My goal is that they may be encouraged in heart and united in love, so that they may have the full riches of complete understanding, in order that they may know the mystery of God, namely, Christ, in whom are hidden all the treasures of wisdom and knowledge."

Prayer:

"God, encourage [Child's Name] in heart and unite [him/her] in love so that [he/she] may have complete understanding and know You, in whom all the treasures of wisdom and knowledge are hidden." Amen.

20. Proverbs 16:3

"Commit to the LORD whatever you do, and He will establish your plans."

Prayer:

"Lord, may [Child's Name] commit all [his/her] actions and plans to You. Establish and guide [his/her] paths according to your will." Amen.

21. Isaiah 54:13

"All your children shall be taught by the Lord, and great shall be the peace of your children."

Prayer:

"Lord, become the ultimate teacher for [Child's Name]. Fill [his/her] heart with an eagerness to learn, and let Your peace be upon them throughout [his/her] educational journey." Amen.

22. Proverbs 22:6

"Train up a child in the way he should go; even when he is old, he will not depart from it."

Prayer:

"Heavenly Father, help me to train [Child's Name] in Your ways. Give me wisdom and patience as I guide [him/her], and may Your teachings remain with [him/her]." Amen.

Conclusion

Praying these personalized Bible verses for your children welcomes God's wisdom and guidance in their educational journey. Trust in His heavenly assistance and continue to pray for your children, knowing that the Lord is with them as they seek knowledge and insight.

Prayer Journals and Reflections
(Write your ideas, requests, and any revelations you receive)

CHAPTER 6

Prayers for Relationships and Friendships

—◈—

Building healthy relationships and friendships is critical to our children's emotional and social development. Praying for these areas can help bring Godly individuals into their lives and foster solid and supportive relationships. Praying these verses over your children can help them receive God's knowledge and blessings as they interact with others.

BIBLE VERSES

1. Proverbs 18:24

"One who has unreliable friends soon comes to ruin, but there is a friend who sticks closer than a brother."

Prayer:

"Lord, help [Child's Name] to choose reliable friends who will stick closer than a brother or sister." Amen.

2. 1 Corinthians 15:33

"Do not be misled: 'Bad company corrupts good character.'"

Prayer:

"Father, protect [Child's Name] from bad company and help [him/her] to surround [himself/herself] with friends who will encourage good character." Amen.

3. Proverbs 27:17

"As iron sharpens iron, so one person sharpens another."

Prayer:

"Lord, bring friends into [Child's Name] 's life who will sharpen [him/her] and encourage [him/her] to grow in wisdom and faith." Amen.

4. John 15:12

"My command is this: Love each other as I have loved you."

Prayer:
"Jesus, teach [Child's Name] to love others as You have loved [him/her]. May [he/she] show kindness, compassion, and understanding in all relationships." Amen.

---

5. Ecclesiastes 4:9-10

"Two are better than one because they have a good return for their labor: If either of them falls down, one can help the other up. But pity anyone who falls and has no one to help them up."

Prayer:
"Father, grant [Child's Name] friends who will lift [him/her] up when [he/she] falls and who will work together with [him/her] for mutual benefit." Amen.

---

6. Proverbs 12:26

"The righteous choose their friends carefully, but the way of the wicked leads them astray."

Prayer:
"Lord, help [Child's Name] to choose [his/her] friends carefully and avoid those who might lead [him/her] astray." Amen.

---

7. Ephesians 4:2-3

"Be completely humble and gentle; be patient, bearing with one another in love. Make every effort to keep the unity of the Spirit through the bond of peace."

Prayer:
"God, help [Child's Name] to be humble, gentle, and patient in [his/her] relationships, making every effort to maintain unity and peace." Amen.

8. Colossians 3:12-14

"Therefore, as God's chosen people, holy and dearly loved, clothe yourselves with compassion, kindness, humility, gentleness, and patience. Bear with each other and forgive one another if any of you has a grievance against someone. Forgive as the Lord forgave you. And over all these virtues put on love, which binds them all together in perfect unity."

Prayer:
"Lord, let [Child's Name] be clothed with compassion, kindness, humility, gentleness, and patience. Help [him/her] to bear with and forgive others and to always choose love to maintain unity." Amen.

9. 1 Thessalonians 5:11

"Therefore, encourage one another and build each other up, just as, in fact, you are doing."

Prayer:
"Father, may [Child's Name] be an encourager who builds others up and fosters a supportive environment among friends." Amen.

10. Romans 12:10

"Be devoted to one another in love. Honor one another above yourselves."

Prayer:

"Lord, enable [Child's Name] to be devoted to [his/her] friends in love, putting their needs and well-being above [his/her] own." Amen.

11. Hebrews 10:24-25

"And let us consider how we may spur one another on toward love and good deeds, not giving up meeting together, as some are in the habit of doing, but encouraging one another—and all the more as you see the Day approaching."

Prayer:

"God, help [Child's Name] and [his/her] friends to motivate one another on toward love and good deeds and to consistently encourage each other." Amen.

12. 1 Peter 4:8-9

"Above all, love each other deeply because love covers over a multitude of sins. Offer hospitality to one another without grumbling."

Prayer:

"Lord, let [Child's Name] love [his/her] friends deeply and offer hospitality without grumbling, knowing that love covers over a multitude of sins." Amen.

13. Proverbs 17:17

"A friend loves at all times, and a brother is born for a time of adversity."

Prayer:

"Father, provide [Child's Name] with friends who will love [him/her] at all times and support [him/her] through times of adversity." Amen.

14. John 13:34-35

"A new command I give you: Love one another. As I have loved you, so you must love one another. By this, everyone will know that you are my disciples if you love one another."

Prayer:

"Jesus, teach [Child's Name] to love [his/her] friends as You have loved [him/her], showing that [he/she] is Your disciple." Amen.

15. Galatians 6:2

"Carry each other's burdens, and in this way, you will fulfill the law of Christ."

Prayer:

"Lord, may [Child's Name] be there to carry [his/her] friends' burdens, fulfilling the law of Christ with compassion and support." Amen.

16. Philippians 2:3-4

"Do nothing out of selfish ambition or vain conceit. Rather, in humility, value others above yourselves, not looking to your own interests but each of you to the interests of the others."

Prayer:

"Father, let [Child's Name] do nothing out of selfish ambition, but rather value [his/her] friends above [himself/herself] and look to their interests." Amen.

---

17. Matthew 18:20

"For where two or three gather in my name, there am I with them."

Prayer:

"Jesus, be present when [Child's Name] and [his/her] friends gather in Your name, bringing Your guidance and blessings to their time together." Amen.

---

18. Romans 15:5-6

"May the God who gives endurance and encouragement give you the same attitude of mind toward each other that Christ Jesus had, so that with one mind and one voice you may glorify the God and Father of our Lord Jesus Christ."

Prayer:

"God, grant [Child's Name] and [his/her] friends the same attitude of mind that Christ had, so that they may glorify You with one mind and one voice." Amen.

---

19. Colossians 4:6

"Let your conversation be always full of grace, seasoned with salt, so that you may know how to answer everyone."

Prayer:

"Lord, may [Child's Name] 's conversations with friends always be full of grace and seasoned with wisdom, knowing how to answer everyone." Amen.

20. Proverbs 22:24-25

"Do not make friends with a hot-tempered person, do not associate with one easily angered, or you may learn their ways and get yourself ensnared."

Prayer:

"Father, guide [Child's Name] to avoid making friends with hot-tempered or easily angered individuals, so [he/she] may not learn their ways and get ensnared." Amen.

Conclusion

Praying these personalized Bible verses for your children invites God into their relationships and friendships. Trust in His divine wisdom to help them cultivate strong, healthy, and God-centered relationships that will favorably impact their lives and glorify Him.

Prayer Journals and Reflections
(Write your ideas, requests, and any revelations you receive)

CHAPTER 7

Prayers for Emotional Well-being, Peace, and Joy

Our children's emotional well-being, peace, and joy are essential for their health and happiness. Leaning on God's word can help our children find comfort, calm, and emotional strength.

BIBLE VERSES

1. Philippians 4:6-7

"Do not be anxious about anything, but in every situation, by prayer and petition, with thanksgiving, present your requests to God. And the peace of God, which transcends all understanding, will guard your hearts and your minds in Christ Jesus."

Prayer:

"Lord, help [Child's Name] not to be anxious about anything. Let [his/her] heart be filled with serenity as [he/she] makes requests to You in appreciation. Guard [his/her] heart and mind in Christ Jesus." Amen.

2. Psalm 34:18

"The LORD is close to the brokenhearted and saves those who are crushed in spirit."

Prayer:

"Heavenly Father, draw near to [Child's Name] whenever [he/she] feels brokenhearted or crushed in spirit. Comfort and save [him/her] with Your presence." Amen.

3. Isaiah 26:3

"You will keep in perfect peace those whose minds are steadfast, because they trust in You."

Prayer:

"God, keep [Child's Name] in perfect peace. Help [his/her] mind remain steadfast and fully trust in You." Amen.

4. Nehemiah 8:10b

"Do not grieve, for the joy of the LORD is your strength."

Prayer:

"Lord, let [Child's Name] find strength in Your joy. May [he/she] not grieve but be filled with Your divine joy." Amen.

---

5. John 14:27

"Peace I leave with you; my peace I give you. I do not give to you as the world gives. Do not let your hearts be troubled, and do not be afraid."

Prayer:

"Jesus, grant [Child's Name] Your peace that surpasses worldly understanding. Let [his/her] heart not be troubled or afraid." Amen.

---

6. Romans 15:13

"May the God of hope fill you with all joy and peace as you trust in Him, so that you may overflow with hope by the power of the Holy Spirit."

Prayer:

"Father, fill [Child's Name] with all joy and peace as [he/she] trusts in You, allowing [him/her] to overflow with hope by the power of the Holy Spirit." Amen.

---

7. Psalm 16:11

"You make known to me the path of life; you will fill me with joy in your presence, with eternal pleasures at your right hand."

Prayer:

"Lord, make known to [Child's Name] the life path. Fill [him/her] with joy in Your presence and eternal pleasures at Your right hand." Amen.

8. 1 Peter 5:7

"Cast all your anxiety on Him because He cares for you."

Prayer:

"Father, help [Child's Name] cast all [his/her] anxieties on You, knowing that You deeply care for [him/her]." Amen.

9. Psalm 94:19

"When anxiety was great within me, your consolation brought joy to my soul."

Prayer:

"Lord, when anxiety is great within [Child's Name], let Your consolation bring joy to [his/her] soul." Amen.

10. Matthew 11:28-29

"Come to me, all you who are weary and burdened, and I will give you rest. Take my yoke upon you and learn from me, for I am gentle and humble in heart, and you will find rest for your souls."

Prayer:

"Jesus, when [Child's Name] is weary and burdened, may [he/she] come to You and find rest for [his/her] soul, learning from Your gentleness and humility." Amen.

---

11. Isaiah 40:31

"But those who hope in the LORD will renew their strength. They will soar on wings like eagles; they will run and not grow weary, they will walk and not be faint."

Prayer:

"Lord, renew [Child's Name] 's strength as [he/she] places hope in You. Let [him/her] soar on wings like eagles, run and not grow weary, walk and not be faint." Amen.

---

12. Psalm 23:1-3

"The LORD is my shepherd, I lack nothing. He makes me lie down in green pastures, he leads me beside quiet waters, he refreshes my soul."

Prayer:

"Father, be [Child's Name] 's shepherd, ensuring [he/she] lacks nothing. Lead [him/her] beside quiet waters and refresh [his/her] soul." Amen.

---

13. Zephaniah 3:17

"The LORD your God is with you, the Mighty Warrior who saves. He will take great delight in you; in his love he will no longer rebuke you, but will rejoice over you with singing."

Prayer:
"Lord, let [Child's Name] know that You are with [him/her]. Take great delight in [him/her] and rejoice over [him/her] with singing." Amen.

14. Philippians 4:4

"Rejoice in the Lord always. I will say it again: Rejoice!"

Prayer:
"Father, help [Child's Name] to rejoice in You always, finding constant joy in Your presence." Amen.

15. Psalm 55:22

"Cast your cares on the LORD, and he will sustain you; he will never let the righteous be shaken."

Prayer:
"Lord, teach [Child's Name] to cast [his/her] cares on You, trusting that You will sustain [him/her] and never let [him/her] be shaken." Amen.

16. Romans 14:17

"For the kingdom of God is not a matter of eating and drinking, but of righteousness, peace, and joy in the Holy Spirit."

Prayer:

"Father, let [Child's Name] experience the kingdom of God through righteousness, peace, and joy in the Holy Spirit." Amen.

17. Psalm 119:143

"Trouble and distress have come upon me, but your commands give me delight."

Prayer:

"God, even when trouble and distress come upon [Child's Name], let Your commands bring [him/her] delight." Amen.

18. Colossians 3:15

"Let the peace of Christ rule in your hearts, since as members of one body you were called to peace. And be thankful."

Prayer:

"Lord, let the peace of Christ rule in [Child's Name] 's heart, guiding [him/her] to be thankful in all circumstances." Amen.

19. Psalm 28:7

"The LORD is my strength and my shield; my heart trusts in him, and he helps me. My heart leaps for joy, and with my song I praise him."

Prayer:
"Father, be [Child's Name] 's strength and shield. As [his/her] heart trusts in You, let [his/her] heart leap for joy and sing praises to You." Amen.

20. Nehemiah 8:10

"Nehemiah said, 'Go and enjoy choice food and sweet drinks, and send some to those who have nothing prepared. This day is holy to our Lord. Do not grieve, for the joy of the LORD is your strength.'"

Prayer:
"Lord, let the joy of the Lord be [Child's Name] 's strength. May [he/she] find joy in Your presence and share that joy with others." Amen.

21. John 16:33

"I have said these things to you, that in me you may have peace. In the world, you will have tribulation. But take heart; I have overcome the world."

Prayer:
"Lord Jesus, let [Child's Name] find peace in You amidst the world's trials. Fill [him/her] heart with hope, knowing You have overcome everything." Amen.

Conclusion

Praying these personalized Bible verses over your children helps to bring God's peace, joy, and emotional well-being into their lives. Trust in His promises and continue to pray for your children, knowing that the Lord is genuinely concerned about their hearts, minds, and souls.

Prayer Journals and Reflections

(Write your ideas, requests, and any revelations you receive)

CHAPTER 8

Prayers for Character and Integrity

—◇—

Leading a God-honoring life requires developing a solid character and keeping integrity. These prayers will assist our children learn the qualities of honesty, kindness, and righteousness.

1. Proverbs 22:1

"A good name is more desirable than great riches; to be esteemed is better than silver or gold."

Prayer:

"Lord, may [Child's Name] always value a good name and reputation more than wealth. Let [him/her] be esteemed for [his/her] integrity and kindness." Amen.

2. Micah 6:8

"He has shown you, O mortal, what is good. And what does the LORD require of you? To act justly and to love mercy and to walk humbly with your God."

Prayer:

"Father, guide [Child's Name] to act justly, love mercy, and walk humbly with You throughout [his/her] life." Amen.

3. Philippians 4:8

"Finally, brothers and sisters, whatever is true, whatever is noble, whatever is right, whatever is pure, whatever is lovely, whatever is admirable—if anything is excellent or praiseworthy—think about such things."

Prayer:

"God, help [Child's Name] to focus on what is true, noble, right, pure, lovely, and admirable. Let [his/her] thoughts be centered on what is excellent and praiseworthy." Amen.

4. Proverbs 11:3

"The integrity of the upright guides them, but the unfaithful are destroyed by their duplicity."

Prayer:

"Lord, let [Child's Name] be guided by integrity. Protect [him/her] from duplicity and unfaithfulness." Amen.

5. Galatians 5:22-23

"But the fruit of the Spirit is love, joy, peace, forbearance, kindness, goodness, faithfulness, gentleness, and self-control. Against such things there is no law."

Prayer:

"Father, may the fruit of the Spirit—love, joy, peace, forbearance, kindness, goodness, faithfulness, gentleness, and self-control—be evident in [Child's Name] 's life." Amen.

6. 1 Timothy 4:12

"Don't let anyone look down on you because you are young, but set an example for the believers in speech, in conduct, in love, in faith, and in purity."

Prayer:

"Lord, let [Child's Name] set an example for others in speech, conduct, love, faith, and purity, regardless of [his/her] age." Amen.

7. Psalm 25:21

"May integrity and uprightness protect me, because my hope, LORD, is in you."

Prayer:

"God, may integrity and uprightness protect [Child's Name] as [he/she] places hope in You." Amen.

8. Colossians 3:12

"Therefore, as God's chosen people, holy and dearly loved, clothe yourselves with compassion, kindness, humility, gentleness, and patience."

Prayer:

"Heavenly Father, let [Child's Name] clothe [himself/herself] with compassion, kindness, humility, gentleness, and patience as Your chosen one." Amen.

9. Proverbs 12:22

"The LORD detests lying lips, but He delights in people who are trustworthy."

Prayer:

"Lord, help [Child's Name] to be trustworthy and honest, knowing that You delight in such character." Amen.

10. Matthew 5:16

"In the same way, let your light shine before others, that they may see your good deeds and glorify your Father in heaven."

Prayer:

"Father, let [Child's Name] 's light shine before others so that they may see [his/her] good deeds and glorify You in heaven." Amen.

---

11. Titus 2:7-8

"In everything set them an example by doing what is good. In your teaching show integrity, seriousness, and soundness of speech that cannot be condemned, so that those who oppose you may be ashamed because they have nothing bad to say about us."

Prayer:

"Lord, help [Child's Name] set an example by doing good, showing integrity, seriousness, and soundness in speech so that no one can find fault in [him/her]." Amen.

---

12. 1 Peter 2:12

"Live such good lives among the pagans that, though they accuse you of doing wrong, they may see your good deeds and glorify God on the day he visits us."

Prayer:

"God, let [Child's Name] live such a good life that others, even if they accuse [him/her] of doing wrong, will see [his/her] good deeds and glorify You." Amen.

---

13. Romans 12:9

"Love must be sincere. Hate what is evil; cling to what is good."

Prayer:

"Lord, may [Child's Name] 's love be sincere. Help [him/her] to hate what is evil and cling to what is good." Amen.

14. Ephesians 4:25

"Therefore, each of you must put off falsehood and speak truthfully to your neighbor, for we are all members of one body."

Prayer:

"Father, let [Child's Name] always put off falsehood and speak truthfully, recognizing the importance of honesty in [his/her] relationships." Amen.

15. Proverbs 10:9

"Whoever walks in integrity walks securely, but whoever takes crooked paths will be found out."

Prayer:

"God, help [Child's Name] to walk in integrity and find security in righteous living, avoiding crooked paths that lead to trouble." Amen.

16. James 1:22

"Do not merely listen to the word, and so deceive yourselves. Do what it says."

Prayer:

"Lord, let [Child's Name] not just listen to Your word, but also put it into practice, living out Your truths in daily life." Amen.

◆◇◆

17. Psalm 15:1-2

"Lord, who may dwell in your sacred tent? Who may live on your holy mountain? The one whose walk is blameless, who does what is righteous, who speaks the truth from their heart."

Prayer:

"Father, help [Child's Name] to walk blamelessly, do what is righteous, and speak the truth from [his/her] heart, so that [he/she] may dwell in Your presence." Amen.

◆◇◆

18. 1 Chronicles 29:17

"I know, my God, that you test the heart and are pleased with integrity. All these things I have given willingly and with honest intent. And now I have seen with joy how willingly your people who are here have given to you."

Prayer:

"Lord, let [Child's Name] be someone who willingly acts with honest intent, knowing that You are pleased with integrity and test the heart." Amen.

◆◇◆

19. Hebrews 13:18

"Pray for us. We are sure that we have a clear conscience and desire to live honorably in every way."

Prayer:

"God, I pray that [Child's Name] maintains a clear conscience and desires to live honorably in every aspect of life." Amen.

---

20. 2 Corinthians 8:21

"For we are taking pains to do what is right, not only in the eyes of the Lord but also in the eyes of man."

Prayer:

"Father, help [Child's Name] to strive to do what is right, not only before You but also in the eyes of others." Amen.

Conclusion

Praying these personalized Bible verses for your children requests God to guide them in establishing their character and integrity. Trust in His divine wisdom to instill virtues in them, allowing them to live lives that honor and praise Him. Continue to pray for your children, knowing that the Lord is faithful to work in their hearts and lives.

Prayer Journals and Reflections
(Write your ideas, requests, and any revelations you receive)

CHAPTER 9

Prayers for God's Purpose and Calling

◆ ◇ ◆

God created each child with a distinct purpose and calling. Praying for our children in this regard can help them identify and fulfill their divine callings.

BIBLE VERSES

1. Jeremiah 29:11

"For I know the plans I have for you, declares the LORD, plans to prosper you and not to harm you, plans to give you hope and a future."

Prayer:

"Lord, reveal to [Child's Name] the plans You have for [him/her], plans to prosper [him/her] and not to harm [him/her], plans to give [him/her] hope and a future." Amen.

2. Ephesians 2:10

"For we are God's handiwork, created in Christ Jesus to do good works, which God prepared in advance for us to do."

Prayer:

"Father, remind [Child's Name] that [he/she] is Your handiwork, created in Christ Jesus to do good works. Show [him/her] the good works You have prepared in advance." Amen.

3. Proverbs 3:5-6

"Trust in the LORD with all your heart and lean not on your own understanding; in all your ways submit to Him, and He will make your paths straight."

Prayer:

"God, help [Child's Name] to trust in You with all [his/her] heart and not rely on [his/her] own understanding. Guide [him/her] in every aspect of life, making [his/her] paths straight." Amen.

4. Philippians 1:6

"Being confident of this, that he who began a good work in you will carry it on to completion until the day of Christ Jesus."

Prayer:
"Lord, instill confidence in [Child's Name] that You, who began a good work in [him/her], will carry it on to completion until the day of Christ Jesus." Amen.

---

5. Psalm 138:8

"The LORD will fulfill his purpose for me; your steadfast love, O LORD, endures forever. Do not forsake the work of your hands."

Prayer:
"Father, fulfill Your purpose for [Child's Name]. Your steadfast love endures forever; do not forsake the work of Your hands in [his/her] life." Amen.

---

6. Romans 8:28

"And we know that in all things God works for the good of those who love him, who have been called according to his purpose."

Prayer:
"Lord, let [Child's Name] know that in all things, You work for the good of those who love You and are called according to Your purpose." Amen.

---

7. Isaiah 55:11

"So is my word that goes out from my mouth: It will not return to me empty, but will accomplish what I desire and achieve the purpose for which I sent it."

Prayer:

"Father, let Your word spoken over [Child's Name] not return empty, but accomplish what You desire and achieve the purpose for which You sent it." Amen.

---

8. 2 Timothy 1:9

"He has saved us and called us to a holy life—not because of anything we have done but because of his own purpose and grace."

Prayer:

"Lord, remind [Child's Name] that [he/she] is saved and called to a holy life, not because of [his/her] own works but because of Your purpose and grace." Amen.

---

9. 1 Peter 2:9

"But you are a chosen people, a royal priesthood, a holy nation, God's special possession, that you may declare the praises of him who called you out of darkness into his wonderful light."

Prayer:

"God, may [Child's Name] know that [he/she] is chosen, part of a royal priesthood, a holy nation, Your special possession. Let [him/her] declare Your praises, having been called out of darkness into Your wonderful light." Amen.

10. Ephesians 4:1

"As a prisoner for the Lord, then, I urge you to live a life worthy of the calling you have received."

Prayer:

"Lord, urge [Child's Name] to live a life worthy of the calling [he/she] has received from You." Amen.

11. Colossians 1:9-10

"For this reason, since the day we heard about you, we have not stopped praying for you. We continually ask God to fill you with the knowledge of his will through all the wisdom and understanding that the Spirit gives, so that you may live a life worthy of the Lord and please him in every way."

Prayer:

"Father, I continually ask that You fill [Child's Name] with the knowledge of Your will through all spiritual wisdom and understanding so that [he/she] may live a life worthy of You and please You in every way." Amen.

12. Proverbs 16:3

"Commit to the LORD whatever you do, and he will establish your plans."

Prayer:

"God, may [Child's Name] commit all [his/her] actions and plans to You. Establish and guide [him/her] in fulfilling Your purpose." Amen.

13. Isaiah 30:21

"Whether you turn to the right or to the left, your ears will hear a voice behind you, saying, 'This is the way; walk in it.'"

Prayer:

"Lord, let [Child's Name] hear Your voice guiding [him/her], saying, 'This is the way; walk in it,' whenever [he/she] turns to the right or the left." Amen.

---

14. Jeremiah 1:5

"Before I formed you in the womb I knew you, before you were born I set you apart; I appointed you as a prophet to the nations."

Prayer:

"Father, remind [Child's Name] that before [he/she] was formed in the womb, You knew [him/her] and set [him/her] apart for specific purposes You have planned." Amen.

---

15. Psalm 57:2

"I cry out to God Most High, to God who fulfills his purpose for me."

Prayer:

"Lord, let [Child's Name] cry out to You, the God Most High, who fulfills Your purpose for [him/her]." Amen.

16. Romans 11:29

"For God's gifts and his call are irrevocable."

Prayer:

"Father, may [Child's Name] understand that Your gifts and calling for [him/her] are irrevocable. Help [him/her] to embrace and walk in them." Amen.

---

17. Psalm 32:8

"I will instruct you and teach you in the way you should go; I will counsel you with my loving eye on you."

Prayer:

"God, instruct and teach [Child's Name] in the way [he/she] should go. Counsel [him/her] with Your loving eye and guidance." Amen.

---

18. Philippians 2:13

"For it is God who works in you to will and to act in order to fulfill his good purpose."

Prayer:

"Lord, work in [Child's Name] to will and to act according to Your good purpose." Amen.

---

19. Acts 20:24

"However, I consider my life worth nothing to me; my only aim is to finish the race and complete the task the Lord Jesus has given me—the task of testifying to the good news of God's grace."

Prayer:
"Father, let [Child's Name] aim to finish the race and complete the task You have given [him/her], testifying to the good news of Your grace." Amen.

20. 1 Corinthians 7:17

"Nevertheless, each person should live as a believer in whatever situation the Lord has assigned to them, just as God has called them."

Prayer:
"God, help [Child's Name] to live as a believer in whatever situation You have assigned, fully embracing the calling You have placed on [his/her] life." Amen.

Conclusion

Praying these personalized Bible verses for your children engages God in their journey of discovering and fulfilling His purpose and destiny. Trust in His divine plan and keep praying for your children, knowing the Lord has a unique and beautiful destiny for them.

Prayer Journals and Reflections
(Write your ideas, requests, and any revelations you receive)

CHAPTER 10

Prayers for Strength and Courage

Amidst life's numerous hardships and challenges, praying for your children's strength and courage can help them overcome hurdles and develop their faith. Use the following Bible verses to pray for your children's strength and courage.

1. Joshua 1:9

"Have I not commanded you? Be strong and courageous. Do not be afraid; do not be discouraged, for the LORD your God will be with you wherever you go."

Prayer:

"Lord, help [Child's Name] to be strong and courageous. May [he/she] not be afraid or discouraged, knowing that You, God, are with [him/her] wherever [he/she] goes."

2. Isaiah 41:10

"So do not fear, for I am with you; do not be dismayed, for I am your God. I will strengthen you and help you; I will uphold you with my righteous right hand."

Prayer:

"Father, let [Child's Name] not fear, for You are with [him/her]. Strengthen and help [him/her], upholding [him/her] with Your righteous right hand."

3. Philippians 4:13

"I can do all things through Christ who strengthens me."

Prayer:

"Lord, let [Child's Name] know that [he/she] can do all things through Christ who strengthens [him/her]."

4. Psalm 27:1

"The LORD is my light and my salvation—whom shall I fear? The LORD is the stronghold of my life—of whom shall I be afraid?"

Prayer:

"Father, be [Child's Name] 's light and salvation. Be the stronghold of [his/her] life, casting out all fear."

***

5. 2 Timothy 1:7

"For God has not given us a spirit of fear, but of power and of love and of a sound mind."

Prayer:

"Lord, give [Child's Name] a spirit of power, love, and a sound mind, not a spirit of fear."

***

6. Psalm 31:24

"Be strong and take heart, all you who hope in the LORD."

Prayer:

"God, help [Child's Name] to be strong and take heart, placing [his/her] hope in You."

***

7. Deuteronomy 31:6

"Be strong and courageous. Do not be afraid or terrified because of them, for the LORD your God goes with you; He will never leave you nor forsake you."

Prayer:

"Lord, let [Child's Name] be strong and courageous. May [he/she] not be afraid or terrified, knowing that You go with [him/her] and will never leave nor forsake [him/her]."

8. Ephesians 6:10

"Finally, be strong in the Lord and in his mighty power."

Prayer:

"Father, let [Child's Name] be strong in You and in Your mighty power."

9. Isaiah 40:29

"He gives strength to the weary and increases the power of the weak."

Prayer:

"Lord, give strength to [Child's Name] when [he/she] is weary and increase [his/her] power when [he/she] feels weak."

10. Psalm 46:1

"God is our refuge and strength, an ever-present help in trouble."

Prayer:

"Father, be [Child's Name] 's refuge and strength, an ever-present help in times of trouble."

11. Psalm 28:7

"The LORD is my strength and my shield; my heart trusts in him, and he helps me. My heart leaps for joy, and with my song I praise him."

Prayer:
"Lord, strengthen and protect [Child's Name]. As [his/her] heart trusts in You, assist [him/her]. Let [his/her] heart jump with gladness and sing praises to You."

12. Nehemiah 8:10b

"Do not grieve, for the joy of the LORD is your strength."

Prayer:
"Father, may the joy of the Lord be [Child's Name] 's strength. Let [him/her] not grieve but find strength in Your joy."

13. 1 Corinthians 16:13

"Be on your guard; stand firm in the faith; be courageous; be strong."

Prayer:
"God, help [Child's Name] to be on guard, stand firm in the faith, be courageous, and be strong."

14. Isaiah 40:31

"But those who hope in the LORD will renew their strength. They will soar on wings like eagles; they will run and not grow weary, they will walk and not be faint."

Prayer:

"Lord, renew [Child's Name] 's strength as [he/she] hopes in You. Let [him/her] soar on wings like eagles, run and not grow weary, walk and not be faint."

---

15. Proverbs 28:1

"The wicked flee though no one pursues, but the righteous are as bold as a lion."

Prayer:

"Father, let [Child's Name] be as bold as a lion, knowing that [he/she] is righteous in You."

---

16. Zephaniah 3:17

"The LORD your God is with you, the Mighty Warrior who saves. He will take great delight in you; in his love he will no longer rebuke you, but will rejoice over you with singing."

Prayer:

"Lord, let [Child's Name] know that You, the Mighty Warrior, are with [him/her]. Take great delight in [him/her] and rejoice over [him/her] with singing."

---

17. 1 Chronicles 28:20

"David also said to Solomon his son, 'Be strong and courageous, and do the work. Do not be afraid or discouraged, for the LORD God, my God, is with you. He will not fail you or forsake you until all the work for the service of the temple of the LORD is finished.'"

Prayer:

"Father, let [Child's Name] be strong and courageous. Enable [him/her] to do the work set before [him/her] without fear or discouragement, knowing that You are with [him/her] and will not fail or forsake [him/her]."

18. Psalm 18:32-33

"It is God who arms me with strength and keeps my way secure. He makes my feet like the feet of a deer; he causes me to stand on the heights."

Prayer:

"Lord, arm [Child's Name] with strength and keep [his/her] way secure. Make [his/her] feet like the feet of a deer and cause [him/her] to stand on heights."

19. 2 Thessalonians 3:3

"But the Lord is faithful, and he will strengthen you and protect you from the evil one."

Prayer:

"Father, strengthen and protect [Child's Name] from the evil one, showcasing Your faithfulness."

20. Exodus 15:2

"The LORD is my strength and my defense; he has become my salvation. He is my God, and I will praise him, my father's God, and I will exalt him."

Prayer:

"Lord, be [Child's Name] 's strength and defense. Become [his/her] salvation and may [he/she] praise and exalt You."

Conclusion

Praying these personalized Bible verses for your children invites God's strength and confidence into their lives. Trust in His promises and continue to pray for your children, knowing that the Lord is greatly concerned about their ability to remain steadfast and courageous in all circumstances.

Prayer Journals and Reflections
(Write your ideas, requests, and any revelations you receive)

Prayers for Obedience and Honor

—◈—

Teaching children to obey and honor authority is foundational to their spiritual and personal development. Use these personalized Bible verses to pray for your children's obedience and honor.

1. Ephesians 6:1-3

"Children, obey your parents in the Lord, for this is right. 'Honor your father and mother'—which is the first commandment with a promise—' so that it may go well with you and that you may enjoy long life on the earth.'"

Prayer:

"Lord, help [Child's Name] to obey [his/her] parents in the Lord and honor [his/her] father and mother so that it may go well with [him/her] and [he/she] may enjoy a long life."

2. Colossians 3:20

"Children, obey your parents in everything, for this pleases the Lord."

Prayer:

"Father, let [Child's Name] obey [his/her] parents in everything, knowing that it pleases the Lord."

3. Proverbs 6:20-21

"My son, keep your father's command and do not forsake your mother's teaching. Bind them always on your heart; fasten them around your neck."

Prayer:

"Lord, help [Child's Name] to keep [his/her] father's command and not forsake [his/her] mother's teaching. Let [him/her] bind them on [his/her] heart and fasten them around [his/her] neck."

4. Deuteronomy 5:16

"Honor your father and your mother, as the LORD your God has commanded you, so that you may live long and that it may go well with you in the land the LORD your God is giving you."

Prayer:

"Father, help [Child's Name] to honor [his/her] father and mother as You have commanded, so [he/she] may live long, and it may go well with [him/her]."

---

5. Proverbs 13:1

"A wise son heeds his father's instruction, but a mocker does not respond to rebukes."

Prayer:

"God, grant [Child's Name] the wisdom to heed [his/her] father's instruction and respond well to correction."

---

6. Proverbs 1:8-9

"Listen, my son, to your father's instruction, and do not forsake your mother's teaching. They are a garland to grace your head and a chain to adorn your neck."

Prayer:

"Father, help [Child's Name] to listen to [his/her] father's instruction and not forsake [his/her] mother's teaching. Let them be a garland to grace [his/her] head and a chain to adorn [his/her] neck."

7. 1 Peter 5:5

"In the same way, you who are younger, submit yourselves to your elders. All of you, clothe yourselves with humility toward one another, because 'God opposes the proud but shows favor to the humble.'"

Prayer:

"Lord, teach [Child's Name] to submit to elders and clothe [himself/herself] with humility toward others, knowing that You show favor to the humble."

8. Romans 13:1

"Let everyone be subject to the governing authorities, for there is no authority except that which God has established. The authorities that exist have been established by God."

Prayer:

"God, help [Child's Name] to be subject to the governing authorities, recognizing that you establish all authority."

9. Titus 3:1

"Remind the people to be subject to rulers and authorities, to be obedient, to be ready to do whatever is good."

Prayer:

"Father, remind [Child's Name] to be subject to rulers and authorities, to be obedient, and to be ready to do whatever is good."

10. Hebrews 13:17

"Have confidence in your leaders and submit to their authority, because they keep watch over you as those who must give an account. Do this so that their work will be a joy, not a burden, for that would be of no benefit to you."

Prayer:

"Lord, help [Child's Name] to have confidence in leaders and submit to their authority, so their work will be a joy and not a burden."

---

11. Proverbs 3:1-2

"My son, do not forget my teaching, but keep my commands in your heart, for they will prolong your life many years and bring you peace and prosperity."

Prayer:

"God, help [Child's Name] not to forget [his/her] parents' teaching but keep their commands in [his/her] heart, so [he/she] may experience peace and prosperity."

---

12. Luke 2:51

"Then he went down to Nazareth with them and was obedient to them. But his mother treasured all these things in her heart."

Prayer:

"Lord, just as Jesus was obedient to His earthly parents, help [Child's Name] to be obedient to [his/her] parents and bring joy to their hearts."

---

13. James 4:7

"Submit yourselves, then, to God. Resist the devil, and he will flee from you."

Prayer:

"Father, help [Child's Name] to submit to You and resist the devil, knowing that he will flee."

14. Proverbs 4:1

"Listen, my sons, to a father's instruction; pay attention and gain understanding."

Prayer:

"Lord, help [Child's Name] to listen to [his/her] father's instruction, paying attention and gaining understanding."

15. Proverbs 23:22

"Listen to your father, who gave you life, and do not despise your mother when she is old."

Prayer:

"Father, help [Child's Name] to listen to [his/her] parents and not despise them, cherishing their wisdom throughout life."

16. Proverbs 15:5

"A fool spurns a parent's discipline, but whoever heeds correction shows prudence."

Prayer:

"Lord, teach [Child's Name] to heed [his/her] parents' discipline, displaying prudence and wisdom in [his/her] actions."

---

17. Ephesians 5:21

"Submit to one another out of reverence for Christ."

Prayer:

"Father, help [Child's Name] to submit to others out of reverence for Christ, displaying humility and respect in all relationships."

---

18. Proverbs 22:6

"Start children off on the way they should go, and even when they are old, they will not turn from it."

Prayer:

"Lord, guide [Child's Name] on the way [he/she] should go. May [he/she] not turn from Your path even as [he/she] grows older."

---

19. Psalm 19:14

"May these words of my mouth and this meditation of my heart be pleasing in your sight, LORD, my Rock, and my Redeemer."

Prayer:

"God, let [Child's Name] 's words and the meditation of [his/her] heart be pleasing in Your sight, O Lord, [his/her] Rock and Redeemer."

---

20. 1 Samuel 15:22

"But Samuel replied, 'Does the LORD delight in burnt offerings and sacrifices as much as in obeying the LORD? To obey is better than sacrifice, and to heed is better than the fat of rams."

Prayer:

"Father, teach [Child's Name] that obeying You is better than sacrifice, and that heeding Your word is better than any offering."

Conclusion

Praying these personalized Bible verses over your children invites God's guidance in helping them develop obedience and honor. Trust in His divine wisdom and continue to pray for your children, knowing that the Lord is faithful to work in their hearts and lives.

Prayer Journals and Reflections
(Write your ideas, requests, and any revelations you receive)

CHAPTER 12

Prayers for Your Children's Love and Unity

— ◇ —

Praying for your children to love one another and live in harmony is critical for creating a positive and supportive family dynamic. Here are 20 tailored verses from the Bible to pray for your children's love and unity among themselves.

BIBLE VERSES

1. John 13:34-35

"A new command I give you: Love one another. As I have loved you, so you must love one another. By this everyone will know that you are my disciples, if you love one another."

Prayer:

"Lord, help [Child's Name] to love [his/her] siblings as You have loved [him/her]. May their love for each other show that they are Your disciples."

2. 1 John 4:7

"Dear friends, let us love one another, for love comes from God. Everyone who loves has been born of God and knows God."

Prayer:

"Father, let [Child's Name] and [his/her] siblings love one another, knowing that love comes from You and that everyone who loves is born of You and knows You."

3. Colossians 3:14

"And over all these virtues put on love, which binds them all together in perfect unity."

Prayer:

"Lord, help [Child's Name] to put on love, which binds [him/her] and [his/her] siblings together in perfect unity."

4. Romans 12:10

"Be devoted to one another in love. Honor one another above yourselves."

Prayer:

"Father, help [Child's Name] to be devoted to [his/her] siblings in love, honoring them above [himself/herself]."

❖ ◇ ❖

5. Ephesians 4:2-3

"Be completely humble and gentle; be patient, bearing with one another in love. Make every effort to keep the unity of the Spirit through the bond of peace."

Prayer:

"Lord, let [Child's Name] and [his/her] siblings be humble, gentle, and patient, bearing with one another in love and making every effort to keep the unity of the Spirit through the bond of peace."

❖ ◇ ❖

6. 1 Corinthians 13:4-7

"Love is patient, love is kind. It does not envy, it does not boast, it is not proud. It does not dishonor others, it is not self-seeking, it is not easily angered, it keeps no record of wrongs. Love does not delight in evil but rejoices with the truth. It always protects, always trusts, always hopes, always perseveres."

Prayer:

"Father, fill [Child's Name] and [his/her] siblings with a love that is patient, kind, and free of envy and pride. May they honor each other, seek others' good, forgive quickly, and delight in truth. Let their love always protect, trust, hope, and persevere."

7. John 15:12

"My command is this: Love each other as I have loved you."

Prayer:
"Jesus, help [Child's Name] to love [his/her] siblings as You have loved [him/her]."

8. Romans 15:5-6

"May the God who gives endurance and encouragement give you the same attitude of mind toward each other that Christ Jesus had, so that with one mind and one voice you may glorify the God and Father of our Lord Jesus Christ."

Prayer:
"Lord, grant [Child's Name] and [his/her] siblings the same attitude of mind toward each other that Christ Jesus had, so that they may glorify You with one mind and one voice."

---

9. 1 Peter 4:8

"Above all, love each other deeply, because love covers over a multitude of sins."

Prayer:
"Father, help [Child's Name] and [his/her] siblings to love each other deeply, knowing that love covers over a multitude of sins."

---

10. Galatians 5:13

"You, my brothers and sisters, were called to be free. But do not use your freedom to indulge the flesh; rather, serve one another humbly in love."

Prayer:

"Lord, teach [Child's Name] and [his/her] siblings to serve one another humbly in love, using their freedom to honor You."

11. Philippians 2:2

"Then make my joy complete by being like-minded, having the same love, being one in spirit and of one mind."

Prayer:

"Father, help [Child's Name] and [his/her] siblings to be like-minded, have the same love, and be one in spirit and mind."

12. 1 Thessalonians 5:11

"Therefore, encourage one another and build each other up, just as in fact you are doing."

Prayer:

"Lord, let [Child's Name] and [his/her] siblings encourage one another and build each other up every day."

13. Ephesians 4:32

"Be kind and compassionate to one another, forgiving each other, just as in Christ God forgave you."

Prayer:

"Father, help [Child's Name] and [his/her] siblings to be kind and compassionate to one another, forgiving each other as You have forgiven them in Christ."

14. Romans 12:16

"Live in harmony with one another. Do not be proud, but be willing to associate with people of low position. Do not be conceited."

Prayer:

"Lord, let [Child's Name] and [his/her] siblings live in harmony with one another, free from pride and willing to associate with everyone in humility."

15. 1 John 3:18

"Dear children, let us not love with words or speech but with actions and in truth."

Prayer:

"God, teach [Child's Name] and [his/her] siblings to love each other not just with words or speech but with actions and in truth."

16. Colossians 3:15

"Let the peace of Christ rule in your hearts, since as members of one body you were called to peace. And be thankful."

Prayer:

"Father, let the peace of Christ rule in [Child's Name] 's heart and [his/her] siblings' hearts, calling them to live in peace and be thankful."

◆ ◇ ◆

17. Psalm 133:1

"How good and pleasant it is when God's people live together in unity!"

Prayer:

"Lord, may it be good and pleasant for [Child's Name] and [his/her] siblings as they live together in unity."

◆ ◇ ◆

18. Hebrews 10:24

"And let us consider how we may spur one another on toward love and good deeds."

Prayer:

"God, help [Child's Name] and [his/her] siblings to spur one another on toward love and good deeds."

◆ ◇ ◆

19. 1 Peter 3:8

"Finally, all of you, be like-minded, be sympathetic, love one another, be compassionate and humble."

Prayer:

"Father, let [Child's Name] and [his/her] siblings be like-minded, sympathetic, love one another, and show compassion and humility."

20. 2 Corinthians 13:11

"Finally, brothers and sisters, rejoice! Strive for full restoration, encourage one another, be of one mind, live in peace. And the God of love and peace will be with you."

Prayer:

"Lord, help [Child's Name] and [his/her] siblings to strive for full restoration, encourage one another, be of one mind, and live in peace. May Your presence of love and peace be with them always."

Conclusion

Praying these personalized Bible verses for your children invites God's love and unity into their interactions with one another. Trust in His promises and continue to pray for your children, knowing that He wants them to live in love and harmony.

Prayer Journals and Reflections
(Write your ideas, requests, and any revelations you receive)

CHAPTER 13

Prayers for the Future

⊰ ◇ ⊱

We fervently pray for God's best for our children's future as parents. Praying the following scriptures over your children can provide spiritual direction, protection, and blessings for the future. Here are personalized Bible verses to pray for your children's futures.

BIBLE VERSES

1. Jeremiah 29:11

"For I know the plans I have for you, declares the LORD, plans to prosper you and not to harm you, plans to give you hope and a future."

Prayer:

"Lord, reveal to [Child's Name] the plans You have for [him/her], plans to prosper [him/her] and not to harm [him/her], plans to give [him/her] hope and a future."

2. Proverbs 3:5-6

"Trust in the LORD with all your heart and lean not on your own understanding; in all your ways submit to him, and he will make your paths straight."

Prayer:

"Father, help [Child's Name] to trust in You with all [his/her] heart and not rely on [his/her] own understanding. Guide [him/her] in every aspect of life, making [his/her] paths straight."

3. Psalm 37:23-24

"The LORD makes firm the steps of the one who delights in him; though he may stumble, he will not fall, for the LORD upholds him with his hand."

Prayer:

"Lord, make firm the steps of [Child's Name] as [he/she] delights in You. Even if [he/she] stumbles, uphold [him/her] with Your hand."

4. Isaiah 58:11

"The LORD will guide you always; he will satisfy your needs in a sun-scorched land and will strengthen your frame. You will be like a well-watered garden, like a spring whose waters never fail."

Prayer:

"Father, guide [Child's Name] always and satisfy [his/her] needs. Strengthen [him/her], making [him/her] like a well-watered garden, like a spring whose waters never fail."

---

5. Proverbs 16:3

"Commit to the LORD whatever you do, and he will establish your plans."

Prayer:

"God, may [Child's Name] commit all [his/her] actions and plans to You. Establish and guide [his/her] paths according to Your will."

---

6. Psalm 20:4

"May he give you the desire of your heart and make all your plans succeed."

Prayer:

"Lord, grant [Child's Name] the desires of [his/her] heart and make all [his/her] plans succeed according to Your will."

---

7. Psalm 32:8

"I will instruct you and teach you in the way you should go; I will counsel you with my loving eye on you."

Prayer:

"God, instruct and teach [Child's Name] in the way [he/she] should go. Counsel [him/her] with Your loving eye and guidance."

8. Philippians 1:6

"Being confident of this, that he who began a good work in you will carry it on to completion until the day of Christ Jesus."

Prayer:

"Lord, instill confidence in [Child's Name] that You, who began a good work in [him/her], will carry it on to completion until the day of Christ Jesus."

9. Romans 8:28

"And we know that in all things God works for the good of those who love him, who have been called according to his purpose."

Prayer:

"Lord, let [Child's Name] know that in all things You work for the good of those who love You and are called according to Your purpose."

10. Isaiah 40:31

"But those who hope in the LORD will renew their strength. They will soar on wings like eagles; they will run and not grow weary, they will walk and not be faint."

Prayer:

"Father, let [Child's Name] place [his/her] hope in You and renew [his/her] strength. May [he/she] soar on wings like eagles, run and not grow weary, walk and not be faint."

---

11. Psalm 119:105

"Your word is a lamp for my feet, a light on my path."

Prayer:

"Lord, let Your word be a lamp for [Child's Name] 's feet and a light on [his/her] path, guiding [him/her] in all decisions."

---

12. Proverbs 19:21

"Many are the plans in a person's heart, but it is the LORD's purpose that prevails."

Prayer:

"God, may [Child's Name] understand that while [he/she] may have many plans, it is Your purpose that will prevail in [his/her] life."

---

13. Psalm 138:8

"The LORD will fulfill his purpose for me; your steadfast love, O LORD, endures forever. Do not forsake the work of your hands."

Prayer:

"Father, fulfill Your purpose for [Child's Name]. Your steadfast love endures forever; do not forsake the work of Your hands in [his/her] life."

14. Joshua 1:9

"Have I not commanded you? Be strong and courageous. Do not be afraid; do not be discouraged, for the LORD your God will be with you wherever you go."

Prayer:

"Lord, help [Child's Name] to be strong and courageous. May [he/she] not be afraid or discouraged, knowing that You, God, are with [him/her] wherever [he/she] goes."

15. 1 Corinthians 2:9

"However, as it is written: 'What no eye has seen, what no ear has heard, and what no human mind has conceived'—the things God has prepared for those who love him."

Prayer:

"Father, let [Child's Name] come to know the wonderful things You have prepared for those who love You, things beyond human comprehension."

16. Matthew 6:33

"But seek first his kingdom and his righteousness, and all these things will be given to you as well."

Prayer:

"Lord, teach [Child's Name] to seek first Your kingdom and Your righteousness, trusting that all other things will be provided."

---

17. Proverbs 22:6

"Start children off on the way they should go, and even when they are old, they will not turn from it."

Prayer:

"Father, guide [Child's Name] on the way [he/she] should go. May [he/she] not turn from Your path even as [he/she] grows older."

---

18. Ephesians 3:20-21

"Now to him who is able to do immeasurably more than all we ask or imagine, according to his power that is at work within us, to him be glory in the church and in Christ Jesus throughout all generations, for ever and ever! Amen."

Prayer:

"Lord, do immeasurably more than [Child's Name] could ever ask or imagine, according to Your power at work within [him/her]. May Your glory be evident in [his/her] life forever."

---

19. Colossians 1:9-10

"For this reason, since the day we heard about you, we have not stopped praying for you. We continually ask God to fill you with the knowledge of his will through all the wisdom and understanding that the Spirit gives, so that you may live a life worthy of the Lord and please him in every way."

Prayer:

"Lord, I continually ask that You fill [Child's Name] with the knowledge of Your will through all spiritual wisdom and understanding, so that [he/she] may live a life worthy of You and please You in every way."

20. Zephaniah 3:17

"The LORD your God is with you, the Mighty Warrior who saves. He will take great delight in you; in his love he will no longer rebuke you, but will rejoice over you with singing."

Prayer:

"Lord, let [Child's Name] know that You are with [him/her] as a Mighty Warrior who saves. Take great delight in [him/her] and rejoice over [him/her] with singing."

21. Psalm 139:13-14

"For you formed my inward parts; you knitted me together in my mother's womb. I praise you, for I am fearfully and wonderfully made."

Prayer:

Creator God, thank you for wonderfully creating [Child's Name]. May [him/her] always realize [his/her] worth and identity in You, knowing that [he/she] is fearfully and wonderfully created. Amen.

Conclusion

Praying these personalized Bible verses for your children's future brings God's direction, protection, and blessings into their lives. Trust in His promises and continue to pray for your children, knowing that the Lord has unique and beautiful plans for each one of them.

Prayer Journals and Reflections
(Write your ideas, requests, and any revelations you receive)

Reflection Prayer

Dear heavenly Father,

Thank you for the lovely gift of my children. As I turn to Your word to pray for their lives, I ask for Your anointing and presence to surround my prayers. May I always be at ease knowing that You are with and looking over them. Help me to pray diligently and impart Your truths in their hearts. I entrust their lives to Your loving and capable hands. In Jesus' name, I pray.

Amen.

Blessing Prayers for Special Occasions

Special occasions provide excellent opportunities for parents to speak blessings over their children, invoking God's guidance and favor. Blessing prayers are for various milestones and events in your children's lives. Praying these blessing prayers over your children during special occasions invites God's presence and power into their lives in meaningful ways. These prayers affirm your love and support as a parent while entrusting your children's future and well-being to God's care. May these prayers be a source of comfort, encouragement, and strength for you and your children as you journey through life together.

1. Birthday Blessing

Verse for Inspiration: Numbers 6:24-26

"The LORD bless you and keep you; the LORD make his face shine on you and be gracious to you; the LORD turn his face toward you and give you peace."

Prayer:

"Dear Heavenly Father, on this special day, I thank You for the gift of [Child's Name]. I pray that as [he/she] celebrates another year of life, you will abundantly bless [him/her]. May Your face shine upon [him/her] and be gracious to [him/her]. Guide [him/her] with Your wisdom and fill [him/her] with Your peace. Protect [him/her] from harm and bless [him/her] with good health, joy, and opportunities to grow in faith and love. In Jesus' name, Amen."

— ◊ —

2. Starting a New School Year

Verse for Inspiration: Joshua 1:9

"Have I not commanded you? Be strong and courageous. Do not be afraid; do not be discouraged, for the LORD your God will be with you wherever you go."

Prayer:

"Lord, as [Child's Name] embarks on a new school year, I ask for Your blessing and protection over [him/her]. Grant [him/her] strength and courage as [he/she] faces new challenges and opportunities. May [he/she] not be afraid or discouraged, knowing that You are with [him/her] every step of the way. Fill [him/her] with knowledge, understanding, and a love for learning. Surround [him/her] with good friends and supportive teachers, and let this year be filled with growth and achievement. In Jesus' name, Amen."

3. Graduation

Verse for Inspiration: Jeremiah 29:11
"For I know the plans I have for you, declares the LORD, plans to prosper you and not to harm you, plans to give you hope and a future."

Prayer:
"Father, I thank You for [Child's Name]'s accomplishment in reaching this significant graduation milestone. As [he/she] steps into a new chapter, I pray that You lead and guide [him/her] in every decision. Reveal Your plans for [his/her] future—plans to prosper [him/her] and not to harm [him/her], plans to give [him/her] hope and a future. Fill [him/her] with Your wisdom and courage to pursue [his/her] dreams and purposes. Keep [him/her] close to You always. In Jesus' name, Amen."

4. Baptism

Verse for Inspiration: Matthew 3:16-17
"As soon as Jesus was baptized, he went up out of the water. At that moment, heaven was opened, and he saw the Spirit of God descending like a dove and alighting on him. And a voice from heaven said, 'This is my Son, whom I love; with him I am well pleased.'"

Prayer:
"Lord, as [Child's Name] publicly declares [his/her] faith through baptism, I pray that You fill [him/her] with Your Holy Spirit. May [he/she] feel Your presence and hear Your voice saying, 'You are my child, whom I love; with you I am well pleased.' Guide [him/her] in [his/her] walk of faith and let this moment mark the beginning of a life dedicated to You. Strengthen [him/her] to live out [his/her] faith boldly and lovingly. In Jesus' name, Amen."

5. First Day of a New Job

Verse for Inspiration: Colossians 3:23-24

"Whatever you do, work at it with all your heart, as working for the Lord, not for human masters, since you know that you will receive an inheritance from the Lord as a reward. It is the Lord Christ you are serving."

Prayer:

"Heavenly Father, as [Child's Name] begins this new job, I ask for Your blessings and favor. Help [him/her] to work with all [his/her] heart, as if working for You, not just for [his/her] employer. Grant [him/her] the wisdom and skills needed to excel in this new role. Surround [him/her] with supportive colleagues and provide opportunities for growth and success. Guide [him/her] each day and let [his/her] work testify to Your goodness. In Jesus' name, Amen."

---

6. Moving to a New Home

Verse for Inspiration: Psalm 121:8

"The LORD will watch over your coming and going both now and forevermore."

Prayer:

"Lord, as [Child's Name] moves to a new home, I pray for Your protection and blessings. Watch over [his/her] coming and going, now and always. May this new home be a place of peace, joy, and safety. Help [him/her] to adjust well and quickly make new friendships. Guide [him/her] in this transition, providing comfort and assurance that You are always with [him/her]. In Jesus' name, Amen."

7. Starting a New Relationship

Verse for Inspiration: 1 Corinthians 13:4-7

"Love is patient, love is kind. It does not envy, it does not boast, it is not proud. It does not dishonor others, it is not self-seeking, it is not easily angered, it keeps no record of wrongs. Love does not delight in evil but rejoices with the truth. It always protects, always trusts, always hopes, always perseveres."

Prayer:

"Father, as [Child's Name] begins this new relationship, I ask for Your blessings and guidance. May [he/she] experience the love that is patient, kind, and free of envy and pride. Help [him/her] to honor the other person and to build a relationship based on mutual respect, trust, and understanding. May their love always seek truth, protect, trust, hope, and persevere through all challenges. In Jesus' name, Amen."

---

8. Overcoming a Challenge

Verse for Inspiration: Philippians 4:13

"I can do all things through Christ who strengthens me."

Prayer:

"Lord, as [Child's Name] faces this challenge, I pray for Your strength and courage. Help [him/her] to remember that [he/she] can do all things through Christ who strengthens [him/her]. Guide [him/her] in finding solutions and give [him/her] the perseverance to overcome obstacles. Fill [him/her] with hope and confidence in Your power. In Jesus' name, Amen."

9. Special Achievement

Verse for Inspiration: Psalm 20:4
"May he give you the desire of your heart and make all your plans succeed."

Prayer:
"Father, I thank You for [Child's Name] 's special achievement. I pray that You continue to grant [him/her] the desires of [his/her] heart and make all [his/her] plans succeed. Guide [him/her] to use this achievement for Your glory and to help others. May [he/she] always remain humble and grateful, giving thanks to You for every success. In Jesus' name, Amen."

10. Spiritual Growth

Verse for Inspiration: Ephesians 3:16-19
"I pray that out of his glorious riches, he may strengthen you with power through his Spirit in your inner being, so that Christ may dwell in your hearts through faith. Moreover, I pray that you, being rooted and established in love, may have power, together with all the Lord's holy people, to grasp how wide and long and high and deep is the love of Christ and to know this love that surpasses knowledge—that you may be filled to the measure of all the fullness of God."

Prayer:
"Lord, I pray for [Child's Name] 's spiritual growth. Out of Your glorious riches, strengthen [him/her] with power through Your Spirit in [his/her] inner being, so that Christ may dwell in [his/her] heart through faith. May [he/she] be rooted and established in love, grasping the full dimensions of Christ's love, and be filled to the measure of all the fullness of God. In Jesus' name, Amen."

Guided Prayers

⟡

Here are some guided prayers that parents can use as templates. Feel free to customize them according to your family's specific needs and circumstances.

Morning Prayer

Heavenly Father, I thank You for this new day. Please watch over [child's name] as they embark on their journey today. Guide their steps, give them wisdom in their decisions, and protect them from harm. Help [child's name] to be kind, patient, and understanding with others. May they feel Your presence in every moment. In Jesus' name, Amen.

Bedtime Prayer

Dear Lord, thank You for the day that has passed and for the protection You provided [child's name]. As they lie down to sleep, grant them peaceful, restorative rest. Guard their dreams and fill their hearts with Your love and tranquility. Help [child's name] wake up refreshed and ready to embrace a new day with enthusiasm. In Your holy name, Amen.

Prayer for the family

Gracious God, we come before You as a family, humbly seeking Your guidance and protection. Bless our home and keep us united in love and harmony. Help us to support one another and grow closer to You. Fill our hearts with gratitude and grace as we navigate life's challenges together. May Your presence be our constant source of comfort and strength. In Jesus' name, Amen.

—◆—

Prayer for Wisdom

Lord, I ask for Your wisdom and guidance as I parent [child's name]. Please help me make decisions that will positively shape their future. Give me patience and understanding to nurture them in Your path. May Your words and love resonate in our home and our hearts. Thank You for blessing [child's name] in my life. Amen.

—◆—

Prayer for Protection

Heavenly Father, I pray for Your divine protection over [child's name]. Surround them with Your angels and keep them safe from all harm and danger. Guard their mind, body, and soul. Please help them make wise choices and steer clear of temptation. May they always feel Your loving presence and know You are their ultimate protector. In Your name, Amen.

—◆—

Prayer for Gratitude

Dear God, I thank You for the countless blessings You have bestowed upon our family. Thank You for the gift of [child's name], for their joy, laughter, and love. Help us always to remember Your goodness and show gratitude in all circumstances. May we continue to grow in faith, hope, and love. Amen.

Prayer for Strength

Father God, I pray for strength and resilience for [child's name]. Please help them to face each day with courage and determination. When challenges come their way, remind them they can do everything through Christ, who strengthens them. Fill their heart with hope and perseverance. In Your mighty name, Amen.

Practical Parenting Tips and Insights

These are practical parenting tips and insights based on biblical principles you can pray about as you apply them to your family's life. Each of these tips can be a focal point in your prayers, asking for God's direction and blessing as you strive to raise your children in a way that honors Him.

1. Model Christ-like Behavior

Lead by example, demonstrating love, kindness, and forgiveness in your daily actions.

Verse:

"Be imitators of me, just as I also am of Christ." (1 Corinthians 11:1)

2. Pray Consistently

Teach your children the importance of prayer by praying together and encouraging them to pray individually.

Verse:

"Pray without ceasing." (1 Thessalonians 5:17)

---

3. Read Scripture Together

Set aside time to read and discuss the Bible as a family, fostering a love for God's Word.

Verse:

"These commandments that I give you today are to be on your hearts. Impress them on your children." (Deuteronomy 6:6-7)

---

4. Encourage Servanthood

Involve your children in community service or helping others, teaching the value of serving as Jesus did.

Verse:

"For even the Son of Man did not come to be served, but to serve." (Mark 10:45)

---

5. Show Unconditional Love

Reflect God's love by assuring your children they are loved, no matter their mistakes.

Verse:

"We love because he first loved us." (1 John 4:19)

6. Practice Gratitude

Encourage a thankful heart by regularly expressing gratitude as a family and recognizing God's blessings.

Verse:

"Give thanks in all circumstances; for this is God's will for you in Christ Jesus." (1 Thessalonians 5:18)

7. Discipline with Grace

Use discipline as a teaching tool, not just punishment, to guide your children towards better choices.

Verse:

"Fathers, do not provoke your children to anger, but bring them up in the discipline and instruction of the Lord." (Ephesians 6:4)

8. Teach Humility

Emphasize the importance of humility and the value of prioritizing others' needs over one's own.

Verse:

"Do nothing out of selfish ambition or vain conceit. Rather, in humility, value others above yourselves." (Philippians 2:3)

9. Promote Honesty

Encourage your children to speak the truth, emphasizing honesty as a critical aspect of integrity.

Verse:

"Therefore, each of you must put off falsehood and speak truthfully to your neighbor." (Ephesians 4:25)

— ◊ —

10. Cultivate Patience

Teach your children patience by showing patience towards them and explaining its biblical significance.

Verse:

"But the Holy Spirit produces this kind of fruit in our lives: love, joy, peace, patience, kindness, goodness, faithfulness." (Galatians 5:22)

— ◊ —

11. Foster Empathy

Help your children understand and share the feelings of others, as Jesus had compassion for those around Him.

Verse:

"Rejoice with those who rejoice; mourn with those who mourn." (Romans 12:15)

— ◊ —

12. Build Strong Relationships

Nurture strong, supportive relationships within the family, mirroring the unity of the body of Christ.

Verse:

"How good and pleasant it is when God's people live together in unity!" (Psalm 133:1)

13. Encourage Curiosity and Learning

Support their learning and curiosity by showing how God is present in the details of the world around them.

Verse:

"Great are the works of the LORD, studied by all who delight in them." (Psalm 111:2)

14. Value Rest

Teach the importance of rest, emphasizing the biblical principle of the Sabbath and the necessity of renewal.

Verse:

"By the seventh day God had finished the work he had been doing; so on the seventh day he rested from all his work." (Genesis 2:2)

15. Instill Confidence in God's Plan

Help your children trust God's plan and timing, reinforcing that He is in control.

Verse:

"For I know the plans I have for you, declares the LORD, plans for welfare and not for evil, to give you a future and a hope." (Jeremiah 29:11

---

16. Be Quick to Listen, Slow to Speak

Practice active listening to your children, showing them they are valued and heard.

Verse:

"My dear brothers and sisters, take note of this: Everyone should be quick to listen, slow to speak, and slow to become angry." (James 1:19)

---

17. Support Their Talents

Please encourage them to explore and develop their God-given gifts and talents.

Verse:

"We have different gifts, according to the grace given to each of us." (Romans 12:6)

---

18. Teach Financial Stewardship

Introduce the principles of generosity and wise resource management, encouraging tithing and charitable giving.

Verse:

"Honor the Lord with your wealth, with the first fruits of all your crops." (Proverbs 3:9)

---

19. Stay Connected to a Faith Community

Regularly attend church and participate in faith-based activities to surround your family with a supportive community.

Verse:

"And let us consider how we may spur one another on toward love and good deeds, not giving up meeting together, as some are in the habit of doing but encouraging one another." (Hebrews 10:24-25)

---

20. Pray for Wisdom

Regularly seek God's guidance in your parenting journey, praying for wisdom and understanding to raise your children in accordance with His will.

Verse:

"If any of you lacks wisdom, you should ask God, who gives generously to all without finding fault, and it will be given to you." (James 1:5)

Inspirational Quotes

These quotes align closely with spiritual growth, parenting, and the guiding power of prayer and scripture. They reinforce the book's messages while offering parents timeless wisdom from respected voices in the Christian tradition. These quotes underscore the importance of faith, family, and the significance of raising children in accordance with God's teachings. Here are some quotes from well-known authors, pastors, and theologians that can offer wisdom and inspiration.

1. Billy Graham:

"Children will inevitably talk, eat, walk, think, respond, and act like their parents. Give them a target to shoot at. Give them a goal to work toward. Give them a pattern that they can see clearly, and you give them something that gold and silver cannot buy."

Explanation: Billy Graham emphasizes that parents have a significant impact on their children. Parents provide their children invaluable guidance and direction that material wealth cannot replace. Children generally model their conduct after their parents. Therefore, parents' attitudes and behaviors have a significant impact on their children's lives.

2. Charles Spurgeon:

"Train up a child in the way he should go—but be sure you go that way yourself."

Explanation: Charles Spurgeon emphasizes the significance of leading by example. Parents are expected to lead their children in the correct direction and embody and apply the principles they teach. A consistent pattern of words and actions promotes the values parents seek to instill.

---

3. C.S. Lewis:

"Children are not a distraction from more important work. They are the most important work."

Explanation: C.S. Lewis emphasizes that raising children is one of a person's most significant responsibilities. Rather than considering children as a distraction from other work, children should be regarded as the primary focus and priority, reflecting the critical role of parenting.

---

4. Rick Warren:

"The best use of your life is to invest it in something that will outlast it."

Explanation: Rick Warren advises people to focus on leaving a legacy that lasts beyond their lifetime. By engaging in their children's spiritual and moral growth, parents contribute to a permanent influence that extends through generations, aligning with eternal values.

---

5. Elizabeth Elliott:

"The routines of housework and of learning at home provide the backdrop for the real work of parenting: nurturing tender souls and applying God's word to their hearts."

Explanation: Elizabeth Elliott emphasizes that, amidst the daily responsibilities and routines, the primary objective of parenting is to foster children's spiritual and emotional development. It entails incorporating God's principles into daily life, shaping their character and faith.

6. Corrie Ten Boom:

"The wonderful thing about praying is that you leave a world of not being able to do something and enter God's realm where everything is possible."

Explanation: Corrie Ten Boom emphasizes the transformative power of prayer, which redirects our focus from human limitations to heavenly possibilities. Through worship, parents can seek God's intervention and guidance in situations beyond their control, providing hope and assurance.

7. Max Lucado:

"God never said that the journey would be easy, but He did say that the arrival would be worthwhile."

Explanation: Max Lucado reminds us that life, particularly parenthood, can be difficult, but the result is gratifying. It promotes endurance and faith in the face of adversity, fostering a belief in the meaningful and fulfilling outcome that God has promised.

8. A.W. Tozer:

"What comes into our minds when we think about God is the most important thing about us."

Explanation: A.W. Tozer reveals that a person's understanding and perspective of God fundamentally influences their identity and actions. For parents, imparting a genuine and profound awareness of God in their children is critical for their spiritual and moral development.

---

9. Andy Stanley:

"Your greatest contribution to the kingdom of God may not be something you do but someone you raise."

Explanation: Andy Stanley asserts that raising children to be faithful and upright can have a profound impact on God's work. Developing a child's character and faith can have long-term consequences for the world and God's kingdom.

---

10. Dietrich Bonhoeffer:

"The ultimate test of a moral society is the kind of world that it leaves to its children."

Explanation: Dietrich Bonhoeffer emphasizes the importance of societal duty in creating a morally sound and equitable environment for future generations. It emphasizes the communal responsibility of building a society that values virtue and provides a positive environment for children to grow and thrive.

---

11. Mother Teresa:

"What can you do to promote world peace? Go home and love your family."

Explanation: Mother Teresa emphasizes that fostering love and harmony within our families is the foundation for broader peace and harmony. Individuals contribute to a more peaceful and compassionate world by cultivating love and understanding within their own homes.

---

12. J.I. Packer:

"Do I, as a parent, pursue God personally and teach my children that knowing and loving Him is the goal of life?"

Explanation: This quote emphasizes the importance of parents setting a good spiritual example for their children. It encourages parents to prioritize their relationship with God while also actively teaching their children the significance of living a life centered on knowing and loving God.

---

13. Ruth Bell Graham:

"As a parent, my strongest hope is to give my children a sense of God and His love, as well as a sense of the lasting values that He has taught us."

Explanation: Ruth Bell Graham emphasizes the necessity of teaching spiritual principles to children. She underlines that teaching children about God's love and instilling solid moral principles are essential to parenting.

---

14. St. Augustine:

"Faith is to believe what you do not see; the reward of this faith is to see what you believe."

Explanation: St. Augustine defines faith as a conviction in unseen truths, emphasizing that true faith leads to the reality of those ideas. In a parental context, it fosters faith in God's promises to their children, even when they are not immediately apparent.

15. Dr. James Dobson:

"Parenting isn't for cowards. This battle will have eternal consequences. You and I must fight for our children's minds, hearts, and souls."

Explanation: Dr. Dobson cautions about the difficulties that come with parenting, claiming that it takes courage and determination. He emphasizes the importance of parenting in a child's everlasting well-being and advocates for a consistent approach to supporting their spiritual, mental, and emotional growth.

16. John Piper:

"The greatest stumbling block for children in worship is parents who do not cherish the hour. Children can feel the difference between duty and delight."

Explanation: According to John Piper, children are acutely aware of their parents' attitudes about worship. If parents regard worship as merely an obligation, their children will notice. He advises parents to approach worship with genuine enjoyment, which can positively influence their children's attitudes toward it.

17. Francis Chan:

"Our greatest fear should not be of failure, but of succeeding at things in life that don't really matter."

Explanation: This quote encourages people to critically review their priorities and focus on what is essential. For parents, it serves as a reminder to prioritize everlasting and significant endeavors, such as their children's spiritual development, over material prosperity.

18. Ann Voskamp:

"Let your religion be less of a theory and more of a love affair."

Explanation: Ann Voskamp advocates for an emotional and passionate approach to faith, rather than a detached or solely intellectual one. This proverb implies that parents should model their faith as a vital, living relationship, which will naturally persuade their children to do the same.

19. G.K. Chesterton:

"The most important thing for a man is to be able to do his duty towards his own family."

Explanation: G.K. Chesterton believes that an individual's essential duty to their family comes first and foremost. For parents, it involves prioritizing family responsibilities, such as nurturing and raising their children, as the foundation of their lives.

20. Tony Evans:

"Your child is either a mission field or a missionary. The central command of the Great Commission is 'make disciples,' and that begins in our homes."

Explanation: Tony Evans emphasizes that children play a dual role in their spiritual journey: as learners of faith and future evangelists. Parents are reminded that discipleship begins at home, where children are nurtured in their faith or encouraged to share it with others.

Prewritten Letters

These letters can be personalized with individual thoughts and sentiments to create heartfelt messages that your child/children will treasure.

Letter 1

Dear [Child's Name],

You have been a tremendous blessing in our lives since you arrived. Each day with you is a great gift that brings us joy and fills us with gratitude. Our desire for you is that you will mature into the great person God has created you to be.

We envision a future where you embrace your uniqueness, pursue your passions, and remain steadfast in your faith. Know that you are profoundly loved, not only by us but also by our Heavenly Father, who directs your every action.

We have many prayers for you, but most importantly, we pray that you will always find consolation and strength in your connection with God. May His love soothe you; His knowledge leads you, and His promises bring hope.

With all our love,

[Parent's Name(s)]

Letter 2

My Dearest [Child's Name],

Your presence in our lives reflects God's unending love and faithfulness. As we watch you grow, we are reminded of the limitless opportunities that await you. You have a special glow that illuminates the world around you.

We hope you will always find strength in difficult times, joy in the journey, and meaning in your chosen route. You have boundless potential, and you can do great things.

In our prayers, we ask that you be endowed with wisdom and understanding, that your heart be filled with kindness and compassion, and that you seek God in all aspects of your life. May your faith be your fortress and a monument to His glory.

Forever yours,

[Parent's Name(s)]

Letter 3

Beloved [Child's Name],

You are a miracle in our lives; each day spent with you reminds us of God's goodness. Watching you grow is our greatest joy, and nourishing your dreams is our true goal.

Our dreams for you are limitless. We hope you have the bravery to pursue your dreams, the wisdom to learn from each experience, and the faith to recognize God's presence in your life. You make us proud in ways that words cannot describe.

We pray that you walk in the light of God's love, believe in His purpose for your life, and always find serenity in His presence. May you be a beacon of His grace and a channel for His love.

With the most profound love,

[Parent's Name(s)]

Dedication Page

This book is passionately dedicated to the lovely children in our lives, those treasured blessings from God who inspire us to grow, learn, and set an example. May the prayers and scriptures within these pages be a beacon of light for you as you travel through life.

To my beloved child, [Child's Name],

May this book serve as a reminder of the profound love and unwavering faith that surrounds you daily. May these prayers provide you with strength and comfort as you grow in wisdom and grace, and may the scriptures nourish and brighten your journey.

A special note for you:

With all our love,
[Parent's Name(s)]

Conclusion

—◈—◇—◈—

In every stage of parenting, praying for our children with God's word is a solemn duty and a beautiful privilege. Each chapter in this book is a comprehensive guide to interceding in various aspects of your children's lives. This collection of prayers allows us to instill God's word in our children's lives, safeguarding their physical and emotional well-being, guiding them with wisdom, and establishing strong Christian character and faith. These prayers are more than just a collection of prayers; they are an invitation to enhance your relationship with God and your children through an empowering act of intercession.

Let these Bible verses serve as the foundation upon which you consistently present your child before the throne of grace. Rest assured that God, who is loyal and loving, hears our prayers and is always present in our children's lives. May this book be a source of encouragement, comfort, and strength as you embark on raising godly children.

About the Author

Iyinoluwa Kuti, popularly known as Nurse Praise on social media, is a devoted believer, wife, and mother of two who seamlessly integrates her faith into every aspect of her life. With 8 years of experience as a registered nurse, she carries a nurturing spirit and a deep compassion for others, which enriches her interactions professionally and personally. Her profound love for children extends beyond her family. She has been actively involved in children's ministry since her teenage years, offering guidance, support, and spiritual mentorship to young hearts seeking to understand their faith.

Her belief in the divine calling of parenthood fuels her desire to write. She is a fervent believer that God has entrusted parents with the sacred responsibility of guiding and nurturing their children through the teachings of the Bible, and this belief serves as the foundation for her literary work. Inspired by this calling, she wrote "Praying for Your Children Made Easy" as a passionate resource for parents seeking to fulfill their spiritual responsibilities.

In this book, she offers parents practical tools and insightful knowledge to help them establish a solid spiritual foundation within their families. Her works strive to inspire parents to be proactive spiritual leaders in their homes, creating an environment in which faith can thrive and children can grow along their predestined spiritual paths. She is committed to supporting and inspiring families, and she continues to inspire others who want to base their lives on biblical principles.

www.ingramcontent.com/pod-product-compliance
Lightning Source LLC
Chambersburg PA
CBHW021151130626
46554CB00005B/1754